# MAKE BETTER
# STRATEGIC DECISIONS

Every day we hear of serious errors of judgement that result in organisational disaster. Why do seemingly successful businesses, NGOs, or even political parties fall prey to irrevocable governance breakdowns or, worse still, criminal malpractice? By prompting readers to think deeply about strategic decision-making, human behaviour, and cognitive biases, this book offers a disciplined, objective, and thoughtful approach to making better decisions.

Every strategic problem is fundamentally a journey into the unknown, which involves a unique combination of duration, scale, external and internal dynamics, and personal motivations. Rarely is a strategic decision solved by saying, 'If a situation is A, then the solution is B.' The book explores how to develop a strong foundation for problem resolving – rather than simplistic problem-solving – by strengthening competence so that decisions are made wisely. The case of Carillion plc, the second-largest construction group in the United Kingdom that went bankrupt in January 2018, is used to explore how a large and profitable company collapsed so dramatically when it was run by an experienced board and advised by three of the Big Four accounting firms. Professor Jeremy N. White presents a clear strategic toolkit for better strategic decision-making.

This book will appeal to senior managers who are interested in techniques for making better strategic decisions. The lessons from the failure of Carillion plc are applicable to corporate leaders in addition to politicians and those who run not-for-profit organisations.

**Jeremy N. White** is a tech entrepreneur with forty years' experience in Europe and the United States, having taken three of his companies public. He serves on the board of Pepperdine University and is a visiting professor at Bayes Business School in London.

"In this illuminating book, Professor White explores why leaders make poor decisions and provides an extensive toolkit to navigate through the messy realities of making strategic choices. The Carillion case illustrates what can go horribly wrong when executives fail to think through the consequences of their actions."

**Professor Gianvito Lanzolla, Professor of Strategy and Digital Transformation, Bayes Business School, City, University of London**

"Strategic decision-making is vexing, pulling leaders in opposing directions amid growing complexity, change, and uncertainty. Jeremy White's *Make Better Strategic Decisions: How to Develop Robust Decision-making to Avoid Organisational Disasters* is a must-read, offering deep insights and actionable practices to help leaders navigate strategic challenges."

**Marianne W. Lewis, Author of *Both/and Thinking: Embracing Tensions to Solve Your Toughest Problems*; Dean and Professor of Management, University of Cincinnati**

"Jeremy White's book wonderfully does what it says on the tin: it gives a guide to strategic decision-making for leaders in the real world, facing complexity, difficulty, and human frailty. It's based on experience and reality. And it's invaluable for the leaders of the future."

**Lord Chris Smith, former Secretary of State for Culture**

# MAKE BETTER
# STRATEGIC DECISIONS

---

How to Develop Robust
Decision-making to Avoid
Organisational Disasters

*Jeremy N. White*

Routledge
Taylor & Francis Group

LONDON AND NEW YORK

Designed cover image: © Getty Images / Eoneren
Designed cover design: Jeremy Morton Design

First published 2024
by Routledge
4 Park Square, Milton Park, Abingdon, Oxon OX14 4RN

and by Routledge
605 Third Avenue, New York, NY 10158

*Routledge is an imprint of the Taylor & Francis Group, an informa business*

© 2024 Jeremy N. White

*British Library Cataloguing-in-Publication Data*
A catalogue record for this book is available from the British Library

*Library of Congress Cataloging-in-Publication Data*
Names: White, Jeremy N., author.
Title: Make better strategic decisions: how to develop robust decision-making to avoid organisational disasters/Jeremy N. White.
Description: New York, NY: Routledge, 2024. | Includes bibliographical references and index.
Identifiers: LCCN 2023035770 (print) | LCCN 2023035771 (ebook) | ISBN 9781032600659 (hardback) | ISBN 9781032600611 (paperback) | ISBN 9781003457398 (ebook)
Subjects: LCSH: Strategic planning. | Decision-making. | Problem solving. | Carillion (Firm)
Classification: LCC HD30.28. W444 2024 (print) | LCC HD30.28 (ebook) | DDC 658.4/012—dc23/eng/20230731
LC record available at https://lccn.loc.gov/2023035770
LC ebook record available at https://lccn.loc.gov/2023035771

ISBN: 978-1-032-60065-9 (hbk)
ISBN: 978-1-032-60061-1 (pbk)
ISBN: 978-1-003-45739-8 (ebk)

DOI: 10.4324/9781003457398

Typeset in Joanna
by Apex CoVantage, LLC

To Kim, Elliot, Amelia, Adelaide, and Annabel with
gratitude for your tolerant indulgence of
my restless mind.

# CONTENTS

# PREFACE

Carillion plc, the second-largest construction group in the United Kingdom, went bankrupt in January 2018.

It had been a leader in construction with huge engineering contracts in the United Kingdom, Canada, and the Middle East. It had annual sales of over £4 billion and profits of £127 million.

Carillion employed 43,000 people and had pension fund obligations for 27,000 retirees. They were a leading contractor to the UK government, paid consistently high dividends that averaged £75 million a year to their shareholders, and twelve months before the collapse had a market capitalisation of over £1 billion.

When Carillion collapsed, staff lost their jobs, tens of thousands of small contractors lost money, and over £1 billion of shareholder investments were wiped out. The 27,000 pension holders worried about their retirement income, and UK taxpayers had to stump up hundreds of millions.

How could a large and profitable company that was run by an experienced board, advised by three of the Big Four accounting firms, and approved for massive infrastructure contracts by the UK government go bust? Was this sad end caused by some seminal event similar to the meteorite that destroyed the dinosaurs? Was the captain of the ship asleep at the wheel? Or was it the culmination of poor decision-making and management papering over the cracks until there was not enough structure left to support the edifice?

Carillion was not unique in making bad decisions. Every day we hear of serious errors of judgement made by individuals and organisations – from politicians and government agencies to not-for-profits and global businesses. If it weren't for this constant stream of failure, the media would have hardly any news to report. However, by understanding why we make bad decisions, we can learn how to make better ones. Any person or organisation faced with making challenging decisions can increase the chance of success and reduce the possibility of disaster by improving their decision-making skills.

As a practitioner rather than an academic, I have been described as a serial entrepreneur and have enjoyed some successes and many setbacks. When I was twenty, I started my first business in electronic security. The company grew and, after ten years, merged with a complementary security group that had launched on the Alternative Investment Market (AIM), a sort of junior stock market listing for small firms with big ambitions. As that company grew, we moved to the main London Stock Exchange, and that was the first of three businesses I took public over the next thirty years.

From wide-ranging experiences in Europe and the United States, my ideas have evolved about how businesses work or don't. As a young man, I thought that luck wasn't so important. But my thoughts on luck have changed, as they have on many other aspects of business and decision-making.

Throughout my career, I've seen a wide range of management styles, business structures, and market dynamics, as well as businesses led by inspirational people and others for whom it is baffling to comprehend how they rose to the top. I worked with people with integrity and, sadly, some with a blatant lack of it. Much as I wish there were clear rules for what works, I have reached the conclusion that there are no fixed formulas. Some strategies intuitively should work but fail, and some seem like commercial suicide yet persist. However, bad decisions have many common factors, and we see leaders who should know better but who repeatedly make avoidable mistakes. Whether it is the toppling of a prime minister after a disastrous policy decision, the fall from grace of a star fund manager, or the collapse of a large public company, there is – as my school reports frequently said, 'room for improvement.'

The writer and thinker, Professor Charles Handy, wrote that decision-makers 'must learn to follow the scientific method, one used by all scientists when exploring the unknown. They take nothing for granted, question accepted wisdom, have boundless curiosity, and have an unrestricted imagination. They know that nothing is for sure, that any hypothesis can only approximate the truth until something more complete or more accurate comes along. They are therefore bold but humble, respectful of authority but doubtful of its conclusions. They are scientific in their method and philosophical in their purpose, querying the "why" of things as well as the "how." [1]

Work, and our attitude towards it, is changing rapidly. The World Economic Forum in Davos in 2020 at the Future of Jobs Forum identified the likely top skills for 2025. They highlighted three key areas:

1. **Problem solving:** involving initiative, analytical and critical thinking, originality, and creativity.
2. **Self-management:** including active learning and ongoing personal development, resilience, stress tolerance, and flexibility.
3. **Leadership:** working with people, motivating them, and harnessing their talents.

Jobs are increasingly shifting to machines driven by algorithms. The demand for high-skilled workers is increasing, and low-skilled jobs are decreasing. Automation is cheap, efficient, readily available, and not subject to labour laws. For example, I recently noticed that a busy Marks & Spencer food store in central London had twenty automated checkouts and only one staff member helping customers.

At New York's recently redeveloped La Guardia airport, the W. H. Smith's store has no sales staff at all. Customers enter through a turnstile using their credit card and select what they want. When they leave, their card is automatically charged on the basis of what they have taken by utilising electronic tagging. It is a reasonable prediction that this trend of integrated automation will accelerate over the next decade, further eroding the demand for low-skilled labour. We are in the fourth industrial revolution.

The first industrial revolution started in the early 1780s and involved steam and water. The second was around 1870 with the division of labour, electricity, and mass production. The third was in the early 1970s with electronics, information technology, and automated production. Now, we are in the fourth. This revolution encompasses cyber-physical systems where mechanisms are controlled by computer-based algorithms – for example, self-driving vehicles, the Internet of Things, and smart grids. It is disrupting and transforming systems of production, distribution, management, and governance.

Billions of people are connected by smart phones to social media. We have effectively unlimited data processing and storage and are seeing the application of artificial intelligence (AI), nanotechnologies, new materials science, and biomedical advances all at increasingly affordable prices. Payment systems linked to instant credit scoring process billions of transactions daily, and mass distribution allows the physical delivery of products within hours. The return on capital versus the return on labour is shifting rapidly, resulting in an increasing disparity between those who can participate and those who are excluded. Talent will be the critical factor in production, and those who can deliver intellectual capital will be the winners – as will innovators, shareholders, and investors.

The current shifts are having effects on customer expectations, the mobility of skilled employees, and the power of government agencies. Agile management is the new mantra as we change how we work, our views on privacy, ownership versus renting, and increasing personalisation based on what AI calculates we want rather than what we as individuals think we want. The important point is that these shifts need to be part of our strategic thinking as they are enmeshed in the most difficult decisions we have to make. They are explored in greater detail in subsequent chapters.[2]

This book examines decision-making mainly from a business perspective, but the observations and lessons have a much broader application. My hope is that you will be inspired to think deeply about strategic decision-making, human behaviour, and cognitive biases and that you will agree with me that a disciplined and thoughtful approach results in making better decisions or at least fewer mistakes.

# INTRODUCTION

In broad terms, this book is about strategy, strategic thinking, and decision-making. We start with broad questions. What do we mean by strategy? Do we need one? Why is strategic thinking so challenging? Then we will consider the rational model based on the assumption that people think logically, make efficient decisions, and then select the optimum outcome. Behavioural economists don't believe that this is true, and they offer an alternative model founded on what we observe in the real, rather than theoretical, world. Let's call this alternative approach 'behavioural strategy.'

The world is messy. The future is uncertain, largely unknown, and opaque. Most strategic problems are paradoxical. That is, they are contradictory but interconnected, we want both but opposing outcomes. The goal of this book is to be a practical resource, enabling you to gain a deeper understanding of organisational strategy through a fresh perspective and to apply tools to address a broad range of decision challenges.

Our organisations face shifting demands – the lack of clarity and unanimity about which direction to take, different and often opposing views about the problems and likely solutions, and the conflicting and conflicted

DOI: 10.4324/9781003457398-1

interests of stakeholders and individuals. Leaders are constantly diverted from addressing important longer-term challenges because of noisy demands – for example, firefighting disasters, dealing with internal politics, staff turnover, and rapid economic shifts. These daily tensions are exacerbated by constantly changing government policies and the endless outpouring of new regulations.

Every strategic problem is a unique combination of duration, scale, external and internal dynamics, and personal motivations. Rarely is a strategic decision solved by: If situation A, then solution B. The real world is too complex and dynamic. We need to move from a mindset of problem solving to problem resolving because we rarely solve strategic problems. We do not fix them. In fact, trying to fix problems often makes things worse. This book explores how to develop a strong foundation for problem resolving by increasing competence so that we act wisely.

Many of the most difficult and challenging problems we face are paradoxical. Rather than seeing this as a problem, we will discover how a paradox can be turned into an opportunity. Risk, decision-making traps, moral and ethical dilemmas, and the conflicting demands of different stakeholder groups are discussed, and then we examine a range of tools to enable us to strengthen our decision-making skills.

Carillion, the United Kingdom's largest business failure, provides a useful case study that is a handy vehicle to bring together ideas on decision-making, risk management, ethics, and social responsibility. The case is unusual, not because of what happened, particularly, but for the breadth of available information that provides deep insights into how a large company was run, their strategic mistakes, their management failures, and their dysfunctional decision-making.

We will forensically analyse the collapse of Carillion with a large and well-documented case study of that important company that failed dramatically. It is helpful to learn from a strategic failure, in contrast to strategic success. Cases of strategic success ignore survivor bias because failed companies are removed from the sample. There is a wonderful richness in the Carillion story that combines strategy, human failing, greed and fear, market pressure and financial troubles, and the ever-present thin line between reality and delusion, truth and fiction.

Michael Raynor, in *The Strategy Paradox* (2007), wrote,

Most case studies tend to focus on success, who wants to learn the lessons of failure, investigating the secrets of success seems more rewarding than picking through the wreckage of failure. Researchers embrace the idea that by studying winners, they can discern the secrets of success, forgetting that the factors differentiating winners from losers can only be identified by analysing both. Failures are often harder to document, or in the case of failed companies, the organisation is no longer available for study.[1]

A great deal of management thinking and investment advice is based on the premise that people behave logically and rationally. As organisational leaders know, however, the world is rarely logical or linear. People make important decisions often in a haphazard way and driven by biases, short-term pressures, and expediency. We are going to explore an alternative to the assumption that we are rational. Behavioural factors based on behavioural theory explain how the interaction of biases, heuristics, hubris, and a host of human frailties impacts our decisions. We will look at how our irrational behaviour leads us to make poor decisions, and we will discover ways to manage these very human limitations.

At the heart of strategy is taking risky decisions. Risk is a core element of decision-making, and addressing risk is a vital executive responsibility. Often, the best we can do is minimise the number of bad decisions we make rather than try to make consistently good ones. Risk and decision-making are stressful, and we will look at how to manage our natural desire to reduce stress by taking the easy options.

Frequently, the most challenging decisions are paradoxical because we desire elements from two or more opposing options. For example, a business wants to reduce operating costs and improve customer service; the government wants to control public spending whilst improving the National Health Service; or the government wants to provide a safe haven for asylum seekers but deter them from seeking asylum illegally. We will investigate paradoxical decision-making and look at ways of harnessing paradox in order to better understand the implications of our strategic decisions and find more creative solutions.

The Carillion story raises moral and ethical issues. We will explore the strategy implications as organisations move from the view of a firm as a profit-making entity responsible only to shareholders to a contemporary vision that recognises that there are multiple stakeholders who often have expectations in conflict with the traditional model. They all demand and deserve balanced consideration.

Leaders frequently face moral dilemmas. We will look at both moral and legal accountability, the impact of an organisation's culture on ethical behaviour, corporate governance and directors' duties, and the role of auditors and other professionals. This book is largely based on British organisations. Obviously, different cultures and countries have their own interpretations of the correct way of conducting business.

If we can hone our decision-making by understanding common pitfalls, we can make more nuanced strategic decisions and avoid some of the most common errors. We can all sharpen our thinking and decision-making skills. By learning to spot and manage our biases, understanding our leadership weaknesses, and watching for thinking traps that trip us up, we become better decision-makers, which should enhance our organisation's long-term performance. Keep in mind that good decisions need to be defined by whom they are good for and over what time period.

Finally, we will bring together what we have learned about the impact of human frailty on decision-making, and explore tools to help us make more robust and reasoned decisions.

## Note

1 Michael Raynor, *The Strategy Paradox* (2007).

# 1

## CORE QUESTIONS

### Strategy

Only sixty US companies on the 1955 Fortune 500 list are still in the top five hundred today. As independent businesses, 88 percent did not make it, but they were all large, successful enterprises run by determined people who were highly motivated to be winners.

The Fortune 100 company list offers a similar stark picture. From 1966 to 2006, two-thirds of the constituents on that list totally disappeared. Only one-third of those businesses survived for forty years, and just 20 percent of them are still on the top 100 list.[1] The change in fortune for those ambitious businesses underlines how difficult it is to be effective and avoid making bad and sometimes catastrophic decisions. It raises the question as to why poor strategic decisions are so prevalent and how we can be more effective.

Why is strategic decision-making so challenging? We will go into this in much greater detail in later chapters, but the key factor is that predicting the future is difficult, if not impossible. At the heart of organisational strategy is the challenge of making important decisions with uncertainty about what lies ahead.

DOI: 10.4324/9781003457398-2

Our goal is to develop a deeper understanding of the decision-making challenges that are faced by strategic leaders and then start building a toolkit of strategies to enhance our decision-making skills. The objective is to become more effective leaders who are grounded in reality. We will become, in Charles Handy's words, 'thoughtful cynics.'

Good judgement takes time to develop and refine. It is built on a foundation of constant improvement, analysing past decisions, learning from our errors, and observing what has worked for others. It is not an innate skill but one that grows over time with much effort and reflection. Later, we will highlight important factors affecting good judgement and how anyone can sharpen their thinking, their decision-making skills, and their leadership talents.

## What Do We Mean by Strategy?

Does corporate strategy exist, or is it all just management? Is strategy about planning for the future and working out where to take an organisation? Is it understanding where you are and where you want to go by anticipating the challenges or threats to the existing organisation and seeking competitive advantage? Do we just choose new opportunities and then allocate resources? Is changing an organisation's culture or mindset part of strategy, and what role should leaders play in the process?

I hope you will agree that strategy encompasses all the above and more. So, what is a strategic decision? I define it as a decision related to strategic questions that concern long-term objectives and the overall aims and interests of an organisation. The objective is to gain a long-term advantage. Strategic decisions result from the formulation and implementation of major goals and initiatives taken by an organisation's leadership based on consideration of resources and an assessment of internal and external environments. Strategic decisions have significant long-term consequences and, as a result, carry greater risk than ongoing operational changes.

There is a blurred area between the incremental improvements managers make every day and those big strategic actions that can dramatically change, for better or worse, the organisation's long-term prospects. The management writer, Bob de Wit, describes incremental improvement as an iterative process, an endless process of thinking and doing.[2]

The incremental development of an organisation is an ongoing management responsibility, and it incorporates the myriad and often small ways we work to refine how the organisation functions. Over time, these small changes can have a significant impact. A manager at the Swiss World Cycling Velodrome in Aigle, where they have trained numerous Olympic cyclists, told me that they work obsessively on each element of an athlete's performance in order to gain perhaps 1/100ths of a second, a small increment, indeed. However, no enterprise is static. They exist in dynamic environments, and complacency inevitably leads to decline, although this can take a remarkably long time for some organisations.

Operational decisions carry lower risk and are shorter-term. There is always pressure to increase sales and margins, address ongoing competitive pressure, adapt human resources, and become more efficient. That is what we generally understand as management. I am convinced that every organisation can be measurably improved – whether it is commercial, not-for-profit, or governmental. We are losing massive amounts of productivity because of poor resource allocation, short-termism, ignorance, sloppy decision-making, and, sadly, apathy. The potential gains are enormous, but that is a subject for another book.

For an organisation to survive or prosper, there must be constant renewal and refinement. Most commercial companies are under relentless pressure from competitive activity, and this forces an active search for ways to upgrade. Monopolies and oligopolies are somewhat protected from this competitive pressure, and that is why they are often regarded as against the public interest. As we will see in the Carillion case, they were also focused on improvement. What destroyed them in the end was their failure to address critical strategic issues in a timely manner. But let's not get ahead of that story at this stage.

Business performance is typically measured monthly, quarterly, half-yearly, and annually; and shareholders expect to see steady forward progress. If the expectation for growth is strong, and the delivery is poor, executives may start fudging, exaggerating, or lying. That's one reason why we need independent auditors, regulators, and non-executive directors (NEDs). What we expect from NEDs is an interesting issue, and we will consider their role later.

The important point is that strategic actions are highly significant, and they impact the way an organisation operates in the longer term. Strategic actions can create turmoil, carry significant risk, and push us to confront those exasperating paradoxical problems.

## Do We Need an Organisational Strategy?

The environment in which we operate is dynamic, subject to constant change, and often shifts in direction when we least expect it. We can address strategic challenges by taking either a reactive or proactive approach. The alternative is to be blown about like a ship in a storm, hoping that the gods will be kind. Ignoring strategic challenges is always an option. Not making a decision, of course, is a decision in itself, but it is a risky approach and one that certainly contributed to the demise of Carillion. Searching for new opportunities, building skills, and developing resources take time and focus. Rarely do massive strategic challenges suddenly appear, and, as we will see in the Carillion case, the antecedents of disaster are often evident much earlier than is commonly believed.

## Why Is Strategy So Challenging?

Recently, one of my post-graduate students made an insightful observation:

> Corporate Strategy is so multi-faceted and complex you could argue that it is almost not worth doing. In my view that would be wrong. The more you think about your organisation and its environment the deeper your understanding of the dynamics. You move from an inexperienced observer to an expert. But experts still face the challenges of dealing with multiple factors and a constantly changing dynamic environment. We need to understand our limitations and not create a sense of certainty where that cannot exist. It doesn't mean that we cannot make any decisions, but we should avoid a false sense of certainty, Brexit provides a topical example.[3]

Decision-making is limited by time and the pressure to address now issues. As we will discover in the Carillion case, ticking off the easy jobs on a to-do list is the same as focusing on today's issues rather than those of tomorrow. Thinking about the future is problematic – the unknowns, unquantifiable, and unpredictable; and the constant buffeting by changing political, competitive, and economic factors.

Nothing is static. There is always someone who wants to eat your lunch, and that forces us to address change. We are adept at resisting change, especially change that harms our personal prospects, and we will explore how to deal with change and address resistance in a later chapter.

Strategic decisions involve processing complex information, and humans have a limited ability to handle complex problems. We struggle to navigate and disentangle complexity, as will be apparent in the Carillion case. We are also emotional and frequently irrational, and we are swayed by our conscious and unconscious biases, greed, fear, ego, and a host of psychological dynamics that interfere with rational thinking.

Paradoxical decisions are especially challenging and stressful because we want two or more contradictory and connected outcomes. Adding to the complexity, people make decisions in different ways that can be effective for one group and a failure for another. After the decisions have been made, plans have to be implemented. So often, a well-conceived strategy fails because of poor execution or is thwarted by internal resistance to change. We will review the important step of implantation in a later chapter.

## Notes

1  Freek Vermeulen, *Business and the Icarus Paradox* (Boston: Harvard Business Review, March 4, 2009).

2  Bob de Wit, *Strategy: An International Perspective*, 7th ed., 2020 Working Paper 10813 (Cambridge, MA: National Bureau of Economic Research, September 2004), 177.

3  Mylene Joa-Longartt, "EMBA Student Bayes," 2021, https://uk.linkedin.com/in/mylene-joa-longartt-5150b47.

# 2

---

# STRATEGIC THINKING

Strategic issues affect all types of organisations – from financial services to retail, from technology to health care – and include government, the voluntary sector, and political parties.

At the heart of corporate strategy is the challenge of decision-making with uncertainty. We will look at decision-making challenges and consider ways to improve the process by recognising the pitfalls and limitations of the traditional approach. We are going to explore real-world inefficiencies, examine human behavioural issues, review the challenges of managing unpredictability, and learn how we can harness paradox. These are areas that have been underexamined in the past, but that is changing. The emphasis here will be on dealing with real-world complexities.

We will explore why the traditional or academic model used to develop strategy has limited utility, despite being widely taught in business schools and practiced by consultants. We will dissect the flaws in the model and develop an alternative approach that acknowledges the powerful impact of psychology on behaviour. The traditional planning model follows a general

DOI: 10.4324/9781003457398-3

format based on three stages: first, analyse the problem; second, work out the problem and propose solutions; and third, implement and test. That model is neat, structured, too simplistic, and largely unhelpful.

## The Rational Model Towards a Behavioural Approach

In 1936, J. M. Keynes wrote,

> Too large a proportion of recent "mathematical" economics are mere concoctions, as imprecise as the initial assumptions they rest on, which allow the author to lose sight of the complexities and interdependencies of the real world in a maze of pretentious and unhelpful symbols.

Keynes was pointing out that theoretical economic models often do not reflect the real world.[1]

The traditional or business school approach to strategic thinking is based on Rational Economic Theory. According to Nobel Prize laureate Herbert Simon, the Rational Economic model is one that assumes the decision-maker is an economic being who tries to take the maximum advantage by selecting the best or optimum solution to a problem. The model holds a number of assumptions, including that the decision-maker has a clear and well-defined goal, is fully objective, rational and not influenced by emotions, understands a problem clearly and precisely, knows all the alternatives and their consequences, has full knowledge, and can analyse the alternatives intelligently. They can rank the alternatives according to preference and will know which consequence is best. Lastly, they have full freedom to choose the alternative that will optimise the decision. That is a pretty long list of assumptions, and some obvious limitations spring to mind. For example, what happens when we have unclear goals or the problems are poorly defined, and how do we handle vested interests from influential people or groups?

A simple example illustrates the fundamental difference in assumptions between rational and behavioural models. According to traditional economic principles, if we are offered two identical pens and one is less expensive, we will always select the cheaper one. Behaviourists would disagree. In their view, there are many factors that affect the choice between identical products at different prices. For example, one might be better illuminated in a display, or one might be reputed to have been looked at by a famous person.

The rational model is logical and linear, and we can link it to the theory of the Efficient Market Hypothesis (EMH). The EMH theory states that a company's share price reflects all information and that it is impossible for an investment manager to consistently outperform the market, technically called consistent alpha. The idea is that shares trade at their fair value, and the share price represents the intrinsic value of the company. However, the EMH recognises that there are bubbles and overcorrections.

The American economist Fischer Black (1938–1995) said, 'We might define an efficient market as one in which the price is within a factor of 2 of value. These things are approximately true but most professional fund managers under-perform the market.'

The share price of a company should reflect all future dividends from the company discounted to the net present value (NPV). Let's keep this idea in mind when we look at the performance of Carillion's share price and its unpredictable movements.

You are probably wondering where this explanation of the EMH is taking us, but bear with me. The problem with the rational model is that economists get into trouble when they make highly specific predictions that depend on people being economically sophisticated. Economists often believe that most and maybe all behaviour is explained by assuming that agents have stable and well-defined preferences, access to all information, and make rational choices consistent with those preferences. Anyone who has worked with decision-makers knows that this is an implausible theory.

So, what are the defining assumptions of traditional/rational economics? The first is that people optimise. But is it even possible for humans to optimise their decisions, and how could we know if we had done so? The second assumption is called consumer sovereignty, and this is the idea that we choose what is best for us. It assumes, therefore, that we don't choose what is bad for us – for example, smoking or refusing the COVID vaccination. But we know there are powerful elements influencing our decisions, including advertising, fake news, influencers both public and private, our limited self-control, and our wilful ignorance, where we intentionally ignore the obvious. These elements often push us towards choices that are not best for us. The third assumption of rational economics is that our beliefs are unbiased, which is self-evidently not true as everyone has biases. The fourth assumption is that we act in our self-interest.

Rational economics doesn't provide a realistic framework for understanding how decision-makers work and how they develop their organisation's strategy. Most economic decisions are taken by amateurs, and, as we will see, their errors are often predictable. Strategy usually involves dealing with big and complex decisions, and they are taken infrequently so we lack practice. We are going to explore an alternative model based on behavioural economics and psychology.

We will develop an understanding of how bias, human thinking limitations (Bounded Rationality), and attitude towards risk all drive and impact strategic decision-making. On our journey, you will meet important behavioural thinkers, including Herbert Simon, Daniel Kahneman, Richard Thaler, Victor Vroom, Ralph Stacey, and others. Perhaps a better name for this new way of thinking about strategy is to call it behavioural strategy. It is a way of thinking that doesn't replace the traditional tools but, rather, augments them.

Behavioural scientist, Richard Thaler, calls traditional economists 'Homo Economicus.' As I stated, traditional economic theory ignores self-control problems and irrational behaviour. Clearly, however, these behavioural issues are highly prevalent. As John Maynard Keynes wryly commented, 'People will do the rational thing, but only after exploring all other alternatives.'

Let me give you an example. A traditional economist would say that removing an opportunity can never make you better off because having more choices is advantageous. However, a behaviourist would suggest that with too many opportunities we become confused and anxious, and we behave irrationally. That is why estate agents try to get you to choose between only two properties, not twenty.

Behaviourists recognise the importance of human factors. People generally do not like making decisions. They don't like change; they don't like disequilibrium; they don't like the unknown and uncertainty. If you want to make someone uncomfortable, ask them to make a decision. These psychological factors have a powerful influence on the choices we make and how we behave under stress.

## The Traditional Approach to Strategy Development

A common framework for developing strategy is based on the traditional, consulting, or business school model. It is based on a circular process, starting with identifying problems at the broader operational level, then moving to the corporate level, and finally looking at networks. The first step is diagnosing the structure of the problem. Potential solutions are then conceived and, finally, implemented.

That approach has risks. We may identify the wrong problem; think of cause and effect. We may misinterpret the problem; there may be many interrelated problems; we may fail to gather the right information or misrepresent it; we might miss possible solutions or select the wrong one; or we might identify paradoxical solutions. We may implement poorly or generate unintended consequences. So, it's a neat approach that is outlined in the following diagram, but it has significant limitations.

Large modern organisations are extraordinarily complex with strategic challenges impacting multiple levels and dimensions of their activities. There are many ways to view an organisation, including through the lenses of finance, logistics, markets, resources, business units, and geographies, as well as from the perspectives of different stakeholders, networks, and alliances. Humans have limited abilities to process complex information, so it is not surprising that we often make poor decisions when we are overwhelmed with information and options.

Remember that traditional economic and political science models use mathematical modelling to make decisions and are often taught to MBA students. These models assume that there is a solution to a problem. Complex,

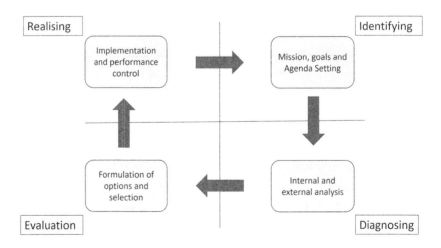

*Figure* 2.1 The traditional model of strategy formulation.

multivariate, and shifting problems are inherently challenging to humans, and there is rarely one correct solution.

Let me introduce some behavioural terms, and later we will explore these in much greater depth. Bounded Rationality, coined by Herbert Simon, recognises that people lack the cognitive ability to solve complex problems. We have mental limitations for juggling many ideas and choices and limited time availability. Decision-making becomes satisficing, meaning that we find a solution that is good enough rather than trying to optimise. Simon offers fascinating insights on human behaviour, and we will look at more of his work in later chapters.

Most of us are uncomfortable addressing complex, challenging, and messy problems. We seek order and clarity. Making complex decisions in an environment of uncertainty is stressful, as we all know when one person is driving and the other is navigating!

When faced with complex decisions and challenging problems under stress, we use rules of thumb or mental shortcuts called heuristics. Simple rules help us make faster decisions. They can be flawed, however, especially when the decision-maker lacks experience. For example, when guessing how frequent something is, we base our estimate on what examples readily come to mind – events that are easy to remember or recent examples – but they may not be relevant or the most appropriate. Another example is following the crowd, which is faster and easier than thinking rationally and understanding why the crowd is moving in a direction. In investing, this effect is known as momentum.

The terms, gut feel and expert intuition, are linked to heuristics. Daniel Kahneman quotes Gary Klein's interviews with a fire chief in the 1970s who pulled his crew out of a kitchen fire, and seconds later the floor collapsed. He didn't know why he did it, but his instinct was correct. Information is processed much faster using intuition, and these skills improve with experience, feedback, and learning from our successes and failures. A challenge of big strategic decisions is that they are taken rarely, so we don't have enough practice to develop strong gut instincts.

You might feel that decision-making, when there is great complexity, has little practical use in planning. But US General Stanley McChrystal, who was the United States Forces Commander in Afghanistan, saw that the value was in the planning process rather than the plan itself. The process of planning makes you think about choices and that, in itself, is helpful.

## Limitations of the Traditional Approach to Strategy

Richard T Pascale, co-author of *The Art of Japanese Management* (1981), challenged the Western view of strategizing and considered the rational analytical approach to be 'myopic and an oversimplification of reality.'

The traditional or consulting model I have outlined follows the logical approach to analyse the problem, examine solutions, select a solution, implement it, and monitor it. All very neat, but at variance with our real-world experience. The real world is messy and unstable. Risk is uncertain, difficult to quantify, poorly analysed, and it is challenging to predict the future with any accuracy. Decision-makers are loaded down with biases and personal hopes and fears.

An organisation is subject to conflicting demands from different stakeholders. Employees want good wages, job security, personal development opportunities, and, in some cases, a well-supported pension plan. Shareholders generally want long-term dividends, business growth, and an increasing share price. Senior executives want high salaries, excellent benefits, generous share options, and pension contributions. They also want a flexible workforce. Customers want efficient services at the lowest possible price. Suppliers want high prices, stability of orders, and growing demand. Governments want successful companies to pay corporation tax, exporting, create jobs, and comply with the law. Local communities want employment opportunities and income from business rates, and specific interest groups such as climate campaigners have their own agendas. This is not an exhaustive list, and there are many variations and overlaps. Clearly, however, a firm cannot meet the expectations of everyone, particularly where demands are paradoxical – for example, low prices and high profits or high wages and high profits.

In addition to conflicting stakeholder demands, there are different or conflicting time horizons. Pension funds might have a 10-year view, and a CEO a year before retirement probably has a different set of priorities compared to a younger person newly appointed to a leadership role. An executive with a large salary and options may have a different agenda than an owner with a large equity stake and a multigenerational perspective.

Organisations are complex systems, and they are subject to nonlinear outcomes in which some apparently relatively trivial event can cast a huge shadow – for example, an event that sets off a cascade of branching histories. Every organisation is in constant flux because of so much variance in business models, leadership styles, culture, and specific situational factors including pressures for change, the competitive environment, company size, different stages of development, black swan events, both good and bad, and market dynamics.[2]

What is the value of the academic model? The model does provide a logical approach and a starting point for thinking about an organisation, but it is only one of many ways of thinking about an entity and its dynamics. The danger, I believe, is in applying the academic model too rigorously because it ignores paradox and thus limits our imagination and insights.

A word on optimising. As a description of behaviour, it is well suited to mathematical techniques and is helpful if problems can be expressed as well-defined models where behaviour can be predicted. Lord King, the former governor of the Bank of England, claimed when he was head of the Bank that he found none of the economic actors were trying to optimise anything . . . shareholder value, social welfare, or household utility . . . and he asked how anyone could have the information to optimise these things anyway and, even if they could, how would anyone know that they were successful?

Many textbooks explain the corporate consulting strategy model; for example, the MBA text, *Strategy Synthesis* by De Wit and Meyer. But as de Witt writes, 'The strategic management literature does not offer clear-cut answers to the question of which corporate strategies are the most successful.'

If it were not enough to think about organisational complexity and dynamics and the pressure from different interest groups and time horizons, we have to overlay the toughest challenge of all, which is trying to predict the future. We're not good at that. Lord King wrote,

> The 2007–2008 financial crisis brought home the intellectual failures of the optimising model to capture the disruptive behaviours that result from confronting an unknowable future. The models of economists, central banks, and the world's largest financial institutions failed to predict the crash.

It is easy to look back and see what happened and find an explanation for problems, as we saw with the House of Commons report on Carillion. But it is infinitely more challenging to be in the moment, face an unknown future, and guess about how things will unfold.

Let me introduce a couple of biases. The Sharpshooter Bias is a handy behavioural trick to define a target after the event. When playing snooker or pool, for example, you say which pocket you aimed for when the ball was disappearing. Hindsight bias – or I knew it all along – is when we overestimate our ability to have predicted an outcome that could not have been predicted.

It is difficult to assess when confidence becomes overconfidence when you are in the moment, but it is much easier to observe afterwards. Neil Woodford, the star fund manager, failed dramatically when he increased his positions when things were going wrong. Woodford's behaviour illustrates the delicate balance between self-belief and self-delusion, characteristics we will see interwoven in the Carillion story.

## Fundamental Uncertainty

The challenge for strategy is predicting the future, and the reality is that we cannot know what the future will bring. We must base our plans on a shaky foundation of uncertainty, whether caused by ignorance and ambiguity, poorly defined problems, or a lack of information, and within the context of the constantly shifting macroeconomy.

Intelligence agencies, including NATO, the CIA, the NSA, the United Kingdom's MI6 and the Military Intelligence Corp., the DGSE in France, the German Bundesnachrichtendienst, and the Italian security service – agencies with incredible resources – broadly failed to predict the speed that the Taliban would overrun Afghanistan. The financial collapse of 2007 and 2008 was missed at which almost every investment bank in the world and the leading economy's chancellors, treasury staff, and state banks. These organisations have access to the world's leading economists and some of the smartest and undoubtedly highest-paid graduates.

We have to function in a world where we are unable to predict such seismic events. And let's not be fooled by the few people who do predict these significant events correctly. Many people make predictions, and most of the time they are wrong, but they have the good sense to keep quiet about them. Be careful not to confuse luck with skill.

We can learn from our mistakes and improve our decision-making, but black swan events do happen more often than we expect and catch us out every time. This book is about how to think more clearly about challenges and decisions, to understand our biases, develop strategies, and hopefully avoid the more obvious mistakes.

## Paradoxical Thinking

I want to give a brief introduction to paradoxical thinking because paradoxical problems are deeply challenging, ubiquitous, and, it might be fair to say, a factor in all strategic decisions. By harnessing paradoxes, we can transform them from stumbling blocks into stepping stones. We will explore this fascinating area in greater detail later.

We tend to see the world as binary and either/or choices – for example, black or white, good or bad, yes or no, right or wrong. However, corporate strategy decisions, and most political and societal ones, are rarely clear-cut choices. In fact, most important decisions are paradoxical because they involve competing choices between two or more desirable but contradictory options.

Paradoxical ideas are those that seem completely rational, independent, connected, and frustratingly contradictory. We want both options at the same time. A paradoxical approach brings together opposing ideas to create new ones. Paradoxical problems cannot be solved; only a satisfactory compromise can be reached. Here are a few examples, and I am sure you can think of many more.

In architecture, we want well-designed, attractive buildings that are well made and last, but, paradoxically, we want construction at the lowest cost and maximum affordability. We want to minimise credit card fraud but don't want to make the transactions so secure that the cards never work. In our case study, we will see how the directors of Carillion faced a choice between the level of dividends paid and the amount of money retained in the business to support other demands. They wanted to both retain cash and deliver to shareholders an ever-increasing dividend. You might agree that both choices are correct, that we want both ends of the polarity and to have our cake and eat it, too. By harnessing both and thinking instead of either/or, there are ways to move forward.

## Paradox and Leadership

Leadership, control, and paradox are three themes that affect all organisations. Leadership is teeming with paradoxes. We want to be in control, and we desire predictability and stability. We believe we are in control, which is often a self-delusion, and others want to believe we are in control. We may be deluding them, but we want others to believe we are in control, for example, to justify why we are well paid. But here is the paradox: We are not in control; we cannot be in control; we do not know what we cannot control; and, of course, we don't know the effects of what we cannot control.

Management control, and I would add political control, is a widely held myth. We believe in management's ability to control and shape the future; however, we operate in a world of randomness and unpredictability. How much performance is due to luck is the great unknown, but I suspect it is much more than we are willing to acknowledge. I will explore the fascinating world of luck later.

We think that brilliant investment fund managers can beat the market, but it is challenging to separate skill from luck. As Warren Buffett famously said, 'Only when the tide goes out do you discover who's been swimming naked.' When the economy does well, politicians claim credit for sound policies, but it is often just lucky timing.

Here is another common paradox of leadership. We want strong leaders with confidence and clear vision, and the rise of populist politicians is testament to that. But hubris, excessive pride or self-confidence, can be both a strength and a dangerous weakness. In January 1944, as the Second World War rumbled on, Operation Shingle was Churchill's much-vaulted amphibious invasion of Anzio in Italy. It proved to be a calamity. There were 43,000 Allied casualties with troops pinned down for four and a half months, and 7,000 soldiers died.

This is what Franklin D. Roosevelt, the President of the United States, wrote: 'The Prime Minister, when fired up with a fantasy, was almost impossible to control. His energy and conviction were exactly how Francis Bacon in 1620 described such leadership,

> A mind, having once adopted an opinion, was wont to draw all things else to support and agree with it. And though there be a greater number and weight of instances to be found on the other side, yet these it either neglects or despises, or else by some distinction sets aside and rejects, in order that this great . . . authority may remain inviolate.'[3]

I claimed that management control is a myth, but it does fulfil an important psychological need. We crave reassurance that someone is in charge and in control.

> We like to endow leaders with super-human qualities and omnipotence – of course we become disillusioned when we find they are far from super-human. Mission statements and corporate vision tag lines support the illusion of control. But mission statements are 'wish driven' founded on what the company would like to become . . . like children saying I want to be a brain surgeon or an engine driver.
>
> (Kay & King, 2020)

## Impediments to Rational Thinking

What are the signs of a robust decision-making process? How a team functions is important, and there should be openness and a meritocratic environment that encourages all members to feel confident in contributing. Of course, a team needs to have competence, clear goals, and a realistic timescale appropriate for the scope of the decision.

Unfortunately, there are a great many impediments to rational thinking, and humans are adept at thinking and behaving irrationally. We will come across many variations of these impediments later, but let's start with fourteen common ones.

1. Humans have limited processing capacity. It is challenging to think through problems with many variables, to quantify probabilities, to process huge amounts of data, and bring that information together to make reasoned decisions. Herbert Simon called these human limitations Bounded Rationality.
2. Often, we have too much data, and on top of that, how do we even know how relevant and robust it is? We are in an information age, and we are overwhelmed. Earlier, I mentioned cognitive heuristics – the simple and efficient rules, hard-coded or learned, that explain how people make decisions quickly. When you are overwhelmed by data, there is a natural tendency to use heuristics, rules of thumb, to escape from the pressure of information overload.

3. Paralysis by analysis. Having too many choices can be overwhelming and can result in a wait and see approach, or just letting the leader decide.

4. Limited time for analysis, discussion, and implementation. Most of us are drowning in today's problems, so tasks such as strategic planning can be put off until things are quieter. Of course, they never are. When an organisation is in crisis or meltdown, as Carillion was for its last few years, it is probably too late to make sensible strategic choices.

5. Decision-making processes are often flawed. Board meetings, for example, are busy events with more topics to address than time available. Not only are there regular operational issues to review, but there are often special problems to discuss such as litigation, compliance, industrial action, financial problems, or even an acquisition. The non-executive directors may not have had time, or the inclination, to carefully review the stack of papers and reports. Depending on the style and power of the chairman, there may be time for careful discussion although, from my experience, there is never enough time. It is easy for a dominant chairman or strong CEO to close uncomfortable discussions and move business along to their preferred topics. As the executives control the flow of information and the agenda, a poor leader can easily abuse their power and stifle constructive debate. On top of these structural problems at large firms, non-executives and even executives rarely have skin in the game, so they have little to gain by rocking the boat.

6. Cognitive maps are mental maps of a problem, and we infer relationships between ideas based on our experiences. We develop these internal mental models and apply them largely unconsciously, and the longer we have been around, the more embedded and rigid they become.[4]

7. Cognitive dissonance. Leon Festinger, an American social psychologist (1919–1989), highlighted the discomfort of holding two contradictory notions and noted that 'We can summon up considerable reserves of wishful thinking and selective memory when we want something to be true, and that helps to restore our mental consistency.'[5] When wishful thinking is linked to our basic instincts of greed and fear, they become powerful tools of the conman.

8. We looked earlier at the role of luck. A test of luck versus skill is whether you can lose on purpose. It is self-evident that the lower the skill level of a decision-maker, the bigger the role luck plays.

9. There are so many highly charged emotions that impact our decision-making. To name a few, there are greed and fear, survival, short-termism, herd mentality, and all the emotions including love, fear, hate, guilt, regret, pride, anxiety, frustration, peer pressure, idealism, power dynamics, and manipulation. With all this swirling emotional pressure, it is remarkable that we make any rational decisions.

10. Presentation over content. There is an aphorism that only the first and last fifteen seconds of a speech matter. Framing relates to how a problem is presented, and we will look at some examples in the section on biases. How we frame our arguments or questions has a powerful influence on decisions, so beware the loaded question.

11. Protecting a carved niche. Nobody votes for a pay cut or a reduction of their power or, as the idiom goes, 'Turkeys don't vote for Christmas.'

12. People resist rethinking their lives work. The great management thinker, Peter Drucker, called that an 'investment in management ego' and cited the resistance to abandon a failed project because too much ego had been invested. We see this at Carillion. The management was so wedded to a policy of increasing dividends that they made it a key performance indicator. But then they were locked in and couldn't abandon the strategy when it was no longer suitable.

13. The illusion of explanatory depth is a common technique used by politicians. We confuse a shallow familiarity with general concepts with a real depth of knowledge. Our knowledge tends to be highly selective and is normally applied to support our position. People fail to notice the logical fallacies in an argument if the conclusion supports their viewpoint and, when shown contrary arguments, will be highly critical of the fallacies in the opposing argument.[6]

14. People confuse their current level of knowledge with past knowledge based on a quite different environment. They have a false sense of expertise that is called earned dogmatism. Watch out for false premises, spoken with real confidence but with minimal understanding of the issues.

The traditional rational or economic model promotes the idea of efficient resource allocation, creating synergy by transferring resources to other business units where better use can be made of them. But the rational model is not properly accounting for these impediments to our thinking and other very human limitations affecting rational behaviour.[7]

It's amazing we are ever rational when you consider the above factors that affect all our judgements. As a final illustration, which of these two £50s affects your emotions more: a £50 parking ticket or letting a £50 discount coupon expire?

## Introduction to Behavioural Economics

A core assumption of neoclassical economists is that agents choose by optimising. Behavioural economists believe that people (agents) rarely optimise in the traditional economic sense. Behavioural economics is not a new idea. Perhaps the first behavioural economist was Adam Smith. In his magnum opus, The Wealth of Nations (1776), 'Man (is) led by an "invisible hand" to promote an end which was no part of his intention.' He added, 'Nor is it always the worse for the society that it was no part of it.'

Smith was talking about, among other things, the behavioural aspects of self-control. He noted that our passions, in economic terms, are shortsighted. We are focused on the short term. Smith also mentions overconfidence, 'the overweening conceit which the greater part of men has of their own abilities' and 'loss aversion,' 'pain . . . is in almost all cases, a more pungent sensation than the opposite and correspondent pleasure.' 'Self-control,' 'the pleasure which we are to enjoy ten years hence, interests us so little in comparison with that which we may enjoy today.' (1759) These are the core ideas of behavioural economics.[8]

Vilfredo Pareto (1848–1923) was another early behavioural economist. 'The foundation of political economy and, in general, of every social science is evidently psychology. A day may come when we shall be able to decide the laws of social science from the principles of psychology.'

John Maynard Keynes (1883–1946), the inventor of behavioural finance, suggests that emotions – he called them animal spirits – played an important role in individual decision-making. In his work, The General Theory of Employment, Interest and Money, Keynes writes, 'Day-to-day fluctuations in the profits of existing investments, which are obviously of an ephemeral and non-significant character, tend to have an altogether excessive and even absurd influence on the market.' (1936) This hypothesis was later confirmed by 1981 Nobel Prize winner Robert Schiller.

Another memorable Keynesian quote warns us about taking unconventional risks: 'Worldly wisdom teaches that it is better for a reputation to fail conventionally than to succeed unconventionally.'

Bucking a trend takes courage. It is hard to be a contrarian thinker, and it is riskier, especially with a bully and dictatorial boss. It is much easier to go with the flow. Alan Greenspan, the famous head of the Federal Reserve from 1987 to 2006, coined the term 'irrational exuberance' to explain stock market bubbles and how it is risky to be a contrarian.

## Behaviourists: Richard Thaler and Others

Richard Thaler, who won the Nobel Prize in 2017 for his work on behavioural economics, highlighted the problem of the rational economic model not reflecting the real world. 'Modelling the world as if it consists of Econs with PhDs is not how psychologists would think about the problem.' Let me introduce a few more important behavioural ideas that we will develop later.

Mental accounting: people are risk-seeking when it concerns losses, and this impacts investment and savings decisions. Keep this in mind when we look at the Carillion case.

Self-control issues: Thaler found that most people realise they have self-control issues but underestimate their severity. We are naive about our level of sophistication at avoiding rational self-control. Who hasn't said, 'Just one more chocolate.' Self-control describes the immediate short-term gratification in service of more important long-term benefits. All theories of self-control are based on the idea of opposing preferences. Starting with Sigmund Freud, many philosophers, psychologists, and economists have conceptualised them as conflicts between different selves within a person. For example, between now self and the future self. The now self prefers consuming a tempting good now, but the future self would regret it. Self-control conflicts are characterised by three criteria: time-consistent preferences, a hierarchy of preferences, and anticipated regret. George Loewenstein, a behavioural economist, argues that the best policies for combating problems of self-control, such as obesity or under saving, are not those that enhance self-control but those that remove the need for it. For example, training yourself to prefer healthy choices.

Fungibility: That is the idea that we can swap one good for another good of the same value, but, in practice, it doesn't seem to happen. For example, people view money from different sources in different ways.[9]

Earlier, I mentioned Herbert Simon's idea of Bounded Rationality, where an individual's ability to process large amounts of information and optimise decisions is limited. Thaler expanded on Simon's concept of Bounded Rationality in his work on nudging us to make better decisions.

Kahneman and Tversky developed Prospect Theory, showing that decisions are based on potential losses and gains, and we will learn more about this important theory and its application to decision-making later.[10]

## Notes

1 John Maynard Keynes, *The General Theory of Employment, Interest and Money* (Cambridge: Harcourt, Brace and Company, 1936).

2 Nassim Nicholas Taleb, *The Black Swan: The Impact of the Highly Improbable* (2008).

3 Nigel Hamilton, *War and Peace: FDR's Final Odyssey: D-Day to Yalta, 1943–1945*, 205. Anzio. The President's inviolate attitude.

4 Bob de Wit, *Strategy Synthesis* (2010), 32.

5 Tim Hartford, *FT*, November 17, 2018.

6 David Robson, *The Intelligence Trap: Why Smart People Do Stupid Things* (New York: Hodder and Stoughton, June 2019).

7 de Wit, *Strategy Synthesis*, 117.

8 Richard Thaler, "Behavioural Economics: Past, Present, and Future," Ryserson Lecture, 2018, https://www.exploring-economics.org/en/discover/richard-thaler-on-behavioral-economics-past-pre/.

9 Richard Thaler, "Anomalies: Saving, Fungibility, and Mental Accounts," *Journal of Economic Perspectives* 4, no. 1 (Winter 1990).

10 www.behaviouraleconomics.com; Joachim Vosgerau, "Exerting Self Control Does Not Equal Sacrificing Pleasure," November 2019, https://www.research gate.net/publication/336677575_Exerting_Self-Control_Sacrificing_Pleasure.

# 3

# CARILLION PLC

'Ignorance more frequently begets confidence than does knowledge.'
— Charles Darwin, *The Descent of Man* (1871)

The collapse of Carillion plc was one of the United Kingdom's largest corporate failures. On 15 January 2018, after a series of profit warnings a few months earlier, the company announced that it was entering compulsory liquidation. Why did one of the United Kingdom's largest construction groups collapse into bankruptcy less than a year after delivering record results?

There is a difference between a puzzle and a mystery. A puzzle has a well-defined set of rules and a single solution. Mysteries don't have such clarity, and they don't have an objectively correct solution. We approach mysteries by asking, 'What is going on here?'

Keep the difference in mind as we dig into the mystery of why Carillion went bust. We must also remember that we are trying to understand something by looking backwards, searching for the cause of the problems in the outcome, and finding an explanation that fits, but correlation does not

DOI: 10.4324/9781003457398-4

imply causation. For example, we might say that Carillion failed because of weak leadership, but there are many firms with weak leadership that don't fail. The risks of causal thinking, the process of identifying the relationship between cause and effect, and the illusion of understanding a problem post hoc are evident as we dig into this fascinating case.

Carillion was winning major government contracts; they issued bullish statements; and they continued to pay an ever-increasing dividend. Two months before their collapse, the Cabinet Office signed off on multimillion-pound projects with Carillion. The company was audited by one of the big four accounting firms and used consulting services from two of the others. The group had a massive forward order book and a long history of major project delivery.

There are lots of clues, and I want to postulate why this long-established, well-respected, supposedly profitable, £2 billion market-cap, dividend-paying, and trusted company suddenly went bust. Carillion's last audited accounts came out in March 2017, nine months before they collapsed. Their vision tag line said, 'Making tomorrow a better place.'

The House of Commons investigation into the Carillion collapse described it as, 'An example of vicious cycles of poor decision-making.' The case allows us to dive into the limitations of the rational model and to see the links between theory and practice.

Carillion plc was the largest trading liquidation ever held in the United Kingdom. What makes the case so interesting is not only its complexity and twists and turns but also the unprecedented amount of information available from the House of Commons (HoC) report. In addition, we have the internal consultant reports from Ernst & Young, the full accounts of a major quoted company audited by KPMG, extensive media coverage, and a government monitoring report.

Using the case, we will review a series of major corporate strategic decisions, try to interpret the outcomes, and consider some of the many factors that led to successes but ultimately failure. From the trove of public information, we can examine the internal workings of a large operation that was dominated by a few senior executives.

Carillion was the second-largest construction company in the United Kingdom with 43,000 employees, of whom 19,000 were in the United Kingdom. Many more were employed in the supply chains. The company was a major strategic supplier to the UK government, which accounted for 38 percent of its business and was spread over an estimated 420 to 450 live contracts. Carillion inherited, mostly through acquisitions, 27,000 pension recipients on defined benefit schemes. The company had notable contracts in the Middle East and Canada and ran over 5,000 apprenticeships.

## The Construction Sector

The top UK construction company by turnover in 2017 was Balfour Beatty, established in 1872, which was the industry leader with a turnover of £8.7 billion, pre-tax profits of £8 million, and a profit margin of just 0.1 percent. The second largest was Carillion, with a turnover of £5.2 billion, a pre-tax profit of £147 million, and a margin of 2.8 percent. Keir Group had a turnover of £4.2 billion and pre-tax losses of £15 million. Interserve's turnover was £3.7 billion with pre-tax losses of £76.4 million. In the fifth place, Morgan Sindall plc had a turnover of £2.6 billion, pre-tax profits of £44 million, and margin of 1.7 percent.

Carillion claimed to be making more profit than the others in the top five UK construction companies, but its accounts also stated they were making more money than the United Kingdom's top twenty-seven largest construction companies combined – £146.7 million versus £142.1 million.[1] What might you conclude from that? Why should the Carillion team have been so much cleverer than everyone else in delivering more profits than all their main competitors combined? Or were the profits an illusion based on accounting sleights of hand, or worse? We will find the answers soon enough.

## Carillion Plc

The story of Carillion goes back to 1999, when the business was demerged from Tarmac. The business grew quickly, expanding from construction into services and facilities management. In 2014, fifteen years after the demerger, Carillion had grown through acquisitions and aggressive growth to become one of the United Kingdom's biggest construction firms. In that year, perhaps because of management's fear of mounting problems, the board attempted a £3 billion merger with Balfour Beatty, which was the largest company in the sector at the time. Perhaps the failed acquisition or merger was a last-ditch attempt to face up to the challenges that were overwhelming the executives. Or was Carillion in denial about their precarious situation and didn't try hard enough to push the merger through?

In August 2014, *The Guardian* newspaper asked, 'Should the market have recognized the Balfour Beatty deal as a warning signal?'[2] Balfour later made this statement, 'Cost savings driven by shrinking the business should not be confused with synergies.' Although the deal never went ahead, Balfour Beatty continued to be an important partner with Carillion on several large contracts. Balfour Beatty was hit hard in January 2018 when Carillion went bankrupt, taking a £45 million loss on three joint ventures with Carillion: major road projects in Aberdeenshire, Cambridgeshire, and northwest England. After the bankruptcy, they took over many of the joint venture arrangements and, presumably, recouped some of their losses.

Carillion's rapid growth strategy was built on acquisitions. The key acquisitions in 2006 included Mowlem, a smaller UK rival, acquired for £350 million, adding £431 million of goodwill to its balance sheet. In 2008, Carillion purchased Alfred McAlpine, a UK-listed construction company, for £565 million, adding £615 million of intangible goodwill to their balance sheet. Eaga, a UK energy services provider, was purchased in 2011 for £298 million, adding £329 million of goodwill. A competitor at the time looked at the deal and considered Eaga to be worth just £25 million.

Eaga is a poignant story. It was in the heating and renewable energy sector and, prior to the Carillion acquisition, made profits of £31 million. Following a change in government policy, Eaga plunged into losses for five years, resulting in an eventual write-off of £298 million. Despite the immediate and continuing losses at Eaga, Carillion's accounts continued to record the £329 million goodwill, and it was not reduced for five years.[3]

Other acquisitions include Bouchier in 2012, Rokstad and John Laing Facilities in 2014, and a Canadian facilities management business in 2016.

According to Civil Service World, Carillion was working on 450 public sector contracts, many of which had been delayed or had seen cost increases. Those included the £475 million Midland Metropolitan Hospital in Sandwell and a £355 million Royal Liverpool Hospital project that included design, build, and facilities management, as well as portering services but excluded anything clinical. The Aberdeen bypass contract was worth an estimated £745 million, and another road project contract for the Lincoln Eastern bypass was worth £155 million.[45]

About 45 percent of Carillion's UK income came from public sector projects. Remarkably, the government awarded £2 billion worth of contracts after the second profit warning in 2017, including a £1.3 billion HS2 rail infrastructure contract just twenty-one days after the company issued a massive profit warning. Carillion became the largest corporate failure dealt with by the Official Receiver.

The Royal Liverpool Hospital was delayed for five years and opened in late 2022. Costs have risen from £350 million to an estimated £1 billion. Serious defects have been uncovered in the concrete beams, and the new contractor, Laing O'Rourke, found the building has been fitted with unsafe external cladding. The project supposedly was on the verge of completion when construction stopped in 2018.

At the Midland Metropolitan Hospital in Sandwell, Birmingham, work stopped on the £475 million contract on 15 January 2018. The project was supposedly two-thirds complete, but a year later Balfour Beatty took over the contract, and now the hospital plans to open by 2024. The costs of the hospital are now estimated to be £1 billion, a massive unbudgeted loss for taxpayers.

Carillion's problems were well hidden. The company's audited results showed steady annual revenue between £4 billion and 5 billion from 2011 to 2016. In December 2015, the company's market capitalisation was £2 billion. A year later, it had fallen by 40 percent to £1.2 billion, and by January 2018, it was zero. Shareholders, suppliers, and subcontractors were left with nothing.

## Collapse

The major collapse of a public company is a rare event. Carillion entered compulsory liquidation on 15 January 2018, announcing the forced closure on the London Stock Exchange. The press release said,

> Despite considerable efforts, those discussions (with its bankers) have not been successful, and the board of Carillion has therefore concluded that it had no choice but to take steps to enter compulsory liquidation with immediate effect. An application was made to the High Court for a compulsory liquidation of Carillion before opening of business today and an order has been granted to appoint the Official Receiver as the liquidator of Carillion. We anticipate that the Official Receiver will make an application to the High Court for PricewaterhouseCoopers LLP to be appointed as Special Managers, to act on behalf of the Official Receiver, and we further anticipate that an order will be granted to that effect.

Dave Chapman, the Government's Official Receiver, added, 'Carillion is the largest ever trading liquidation in the UK.'

At the time of liquidation, Carillion owed £1.3 billion to banks, had an estimated £800 million pension deficit, and only £29 million in cash. All shareholder funds valued at £1.2 billion were lost.[6] Private investors were the hardest hit. The 27,000 members of the defined benefit pension scheme were affected, and 30,000 largely small suppliers, subcontractors, and short-term contractors were owed £2 billion. The UK government committed £150 million to keep essential services running, but no one knows the true cost to the taxpayer of the collapse.

How can a company that for so long boasted an unblemished record of progress, an ever-increasing dividend, and was supported by optimistic statements from its board suddenly announce its collapse only a few months after issuing its annual report? As I mentioned earlier, there is an unparalleled amount of internal information available for examination, so we can look at Carillion's strategy, decision-making process, managerial failings, and behavioural dynamics.

In trying to unravel the mystery behind the collapse, there are numerous factors to consider. Carillion undertook multiple acquisitions that brought significant pension liabilities that were difficult to quantify. The company had just two senior executives on the group board who, by all accounts, were out of their depth. There was arrogance, hubris, and denial combined with a head-in-the-sand approach to serious problems that over time resulted in increased accounting fiction and misrepresentation. The board paid lip service to risks and went to increasing lengths to cover up mistakes. There was weak and inadequate supervision by non-executive directors, top accounting firms, and global consultants to add to the mix of impending catastrophe.

It is interesting to look in detail at the timeline of the nine months before the compulsory liquidation on 15 January 2018. Events moved at a rapid pace. On 1 March 2017, the 2016 Annual Report and accounts were signed and published. Just after publication of the accounts, the company executives were in an open period and could sell shares. Richard Adam, the recently retired Chief Financial Officer, sold his shares for £534,000. On 3 May, Carillion held its annual general meeting, and there were no adverse comments. Later in the month, the board, working with their auditors, KPMG, conducted a review of accounting treatment for receivables following concerns raised by Emma Mercer, who had been the CFO of Carillion in Canada.

In the same month, the review concluded that assets had been misclassified but that there had been no misstatement of revenue. Following that review, there was a wider review of contract positions. On 9 June, Carillion paid out a final dividend of £55 million for the year ended 2016.

According to publicly available board meeting minutes from 5 July 2017, the board received news that Morgan Stanley, Carillion's brokers, were no longer prepared to underwrite a cash-raising rights issue. The size of the bad debts was too large for Morgan Stanley's investment committee to sign off. According to the minutes, the directors asked no questions of the Morgan Stanley executive who had delivered the devastating news, and they considered that the broker was being unreasonable. Chairman Philip Green went on to say that they should continue to make a 'positive and upbeat announcement.' On 9 July, the audit committee considered the outcome of the contract review. It was clear that a large provision against contracts had to be made, and the initial estimate was £645 million. Shortly after, that was revised upward to £845 million. That massive revision was barely three months after the publication of the 2016 Report and Accounts, and, to put this loss into perspective, it was similar to the stock market value of the company. A day later, on 10 July, Carillion issued a profit warning regarding 'an unexpected contract provision of £845 million and a comprehensive review of the Group's business and capital structure.' The Chief Executive, Richard Howson, resigned with immediate effect. Within two days, the share price dropped by 70 percent. On 14 July, the Big Four accounting company, Ernst & Young (EY), was appointed to conduct a strategic review with a focus on urgent cost reduction and cash collection, and HSBC was appointed as a new broker. Just three days later, the UK government announced that Carillion had secured a major contract for the building of the new rail network, HS2, for £450 million.

Zafar Khan, who took over as CFO when Richard Adam retired, stood down as group FD on 11 September, and Emma Mercer took over. On 29 September 2017, Carillion issued its second profit warning, and the half-year results show another £200 million profit write-down. On 24 October, Carillion agreed to a deferral of the pension deficit contributions, releasing £100 million unsecured and £40 million secured bank finance. A month later, on 17 November, then just two months away from collapse, there was a third profit warning together with an announcement that the company was at risk of breaching its debt covenants. The share price declined again, losing 87 percent of its value since July 2017.

In December 2017, Kiltearn Partners, the largest shareholder in Carillion, started cutting its losses by halving its stake. By the end of December, finance creditors received an updated cash flow, showing that the company would have less than £20 million by March 2018. On New Year's Eve, Carillion submitted a formal request to the government for support. At the start of the New Year on 3 January, the FCA notified Carillion that it had commenced an investigation into the timeliness of announcements made between 7 December 2016 and 10 July 2017. On 13 January, Carillion wrote to the Cabinet Office, making a final request for £160 million, and two days later received a reply that no support would be provided. The company announced that it had no choice but to enter compulsory liquidation.

## The Collapse and Broad Business Issues

In just three months from the publication of its accounts for 2016, Carillion lost its CEO, the interim CEO Keith Cochrane and announced the write-off of £845 million on three major public-private partnerships: the construction projects for the Royal Liverpool and Midland Metropolitan hospitals and the Aberdeen bypass. The contract provisions rose to £1.045 billion in September 2017 and an astonishing £1.105 billion by January 2018. Did some catastrophic event take place, rather like a meteorite wiping out the dinosaurs, or was the pressure on the business, built up after so many years of management failure, just too great to stop its demise?

The Carillion collapse triggered two parliamentary select committees, an FCA inquiry, accounting regulator examinations, and extensive litigation against the directors, accountants, and other connected parties. The company's auditor, KPMG, faced a claim of £1.3 billion before the High Court by the Official Receiver.

There are broad business issues and themes that are interesting to consider, so let's look at these now.

Carillion operated with slim margins. Their large contracts were complex and difficult to control, and the construction sector, rather like the airline industry, barely permitted large-scale operators to generate adequate returns. The seeds of collapse were sown long ago, however, and the failure was exacerbated by a mindset of optimism and denial.

We are going to examine if the risks could or should have been spotted earlier and whether the accounts captured the risks that Carillion faced.

Were the directors open and honest about the true challenges, and did they comply with their legal and moral responsibilities? Why did analysts and bankers fail to adequately price the risk, and why did investors so misjudge the value of the company? These and a host of other issues raise questions about the company's strategy and management, the adequacy of professional advisers and auditors, and the checks on a publicly quoted company with thousands of shareholders. Perhaps more important is what we can learn from Carillion's collapse and how we can apply these lessons to the way we manage our own organisations.

Carillion was managing hundreds of significant infrastructure contracts in multiple countries with slim margins. The scale and nature of the projects meant that they were difficult to price, control, and deliver. Was the company operating in an overcrowded market that was unable to offer adequate returns for the risks involved? Were the underlying reasons for the collapse initiated more than a decade earlier because of ill-considered acquisitions that carried huge pension liabilities? Did the limited ability of the senior directors compound the problem? Was there a systematic mindset of optimism and denial in collusion with professional advisers and auditors? Could or should the internal and external auditors have highlighted the risks earlier, or did they flag the problems, but the warnings were ignored by management and investors?

A broader question is why the International Accounting Standards and annual corporate disclosures, which these days are extensive, still fail to capture the true risk. Should the standards be enhanced? Why did most fund managers, who are responsible for assessing companies, fail to spot the problems earlier? Did the failure of Carillion come from the top, or were there problems at multiple levels within the business, or was it all just bad luck? Of interest to our investigation, can behavioural finance tools provide earlier detection of systemic risks?

## Carillion Business Strategy

Let's explore some of the policies that drove Carillion's strategy. Constant growth is a key theme mentioned in the report and accounts. There may be nothing wrong with such a strategy if it is realistic, but was it valid in Carillion's case? Carillion operated in a fiercely competitive market; therefore, to achieve constant growth, there would have to be an expanding market, an increasing market share, or a combination of the two.

Carillion boasted a policy of increasing dividends, a so-called progressive dividend policy. Was an ever-growing dividend to shareholders achievable or even possible in a cyclical industry where revenue and profits are impacted by macroeconomic factors?

As the dividends were increasing, so were the company's borrowings. Carillion's debt trebled from 2010 to 2012 and then stayed flat from 2012 to 2016, but that was misleading because Carillion was using off-balance-sheet funding to finance the business. The company embraced a novel form of funding that acted like debt but wasn't classified as such on the accounts. Supply chain factoring or early payment facility (EPF) is a scheme to pay suppliers early in return for a discount and, conveniently for Carillion, was not classified as borrowing but as other creditors. By using that method to fund the business, Carillion was making the company's finances look healthier than they were, although they were not breaking the law. Moody's, the credit rating agency, estimated that £498 million of Carillion's borrowing was misclassified in that way.

Here is an interesting piece of financial history. In late 2012, Lex Greensill of Greensill Capital presented government ministers with an innovative new scheme designed to speed up payments to government suppliers, many of whom were small businesses. Large companies were criticised for forcing small businesses to accept onerously slow payment terms. Small firms, which have historically found borrowing to be challenging and expensive, discovered that supply chain finance was a lifesaving cash-flow facility, although it was expensive. Carillion adopted the Greensill model and, at the same time, extended its payment terms from 65 to 120 days. The suppliers, often small subcontractor firms, were getting paid just as slowly but were having to pay interest on loans.

Another Carillion aggressive accounting policy was stacking the balance sheet with goodwill, which is an intangible asset that arises when a buyer acquires an existing business. The amount of goodwill is broadly the excess price paid for the business over the value of tangible assets. A large goodwill figure on a company's balance sheet indicates that significant amounts have been paid for the non-tangible assets in an acquisition. This is not necessarily a bad thing, but if an acquired business has been overvalued and the goodwill figure is not corrected in the accounts, then the company looks to have more assets than it really does. That was certainly the case at Carillion, where intangible assets of goodwill stood at around £1.6 billion, which represented 35 percent of the company's gross assets and more than double its net assets of £730 million.

Under the rules of accounting standards, the value of goodwill should be reviewed every year; however, the overstatement of goodwill at Carillion was never impaired in its annual accounts. The goodwill number was a fantasy, but it took years before those outside the company found out the scale of the deceit.

The consequences of having an increasing dividend policy, increasing debt, and off-balance-sheet finance forced Carillion to "dash for cash", and cash pressures seem to have been a major factor driving both operational and strategic decisions and draining senior management resources. Richard Howson told the House of Commons committee that he had over six years made sixty visits to Qatar to collect cash. He said he 'felt like a bailiff.' Hardly an efficient use of the CEO's time.

## Growth Through Acquisition

Acquisitions offer a shortcut route to growth but not without risk. The risk comes in many forms. For example, it is hard to know what you are buying; usually you are paying top price, and acquisitions demand significant management resources. In addition, bigger organisations are more complex and, therefore, harder to manage and may be beyond the capabilities of the existing team. If funding comes from debt, then servicing costs increase and are subject to rapid shifts in interest rates. One of the most significant problems resulting from acquisitions for Carillion was the exposure to defined benefit pensions. Such pensions are a liability and require a company to pay retired employees a pension, usually inflation protected, for as long as the retiree survives. The liability can be enormous and is difficult to quantify. Management faces a constant challenge over what are adequate provisions to cover the debt. Future stock market performance and inflation are significant factors affecting the scale of the liability.

The Financial Times columnist, Tim Steer, wrote in The Signs Were There,

Acquisitive companies often do not add shareholder value. Acquisitions offer a rapid way to grow a business, but it is a challenging and difficult strategy. It is difficult, even when buying a quoted company to know exactly what you are buying and to work out what is a fair price to pay. Then after the acquisition the new entity must add at least the value expected or more. Integrating different cultures and creating synergy are difficult even for excellent management teams. Often the motivation for the acquirer is not improvement of their own business but an ego driven urge to become bigger for the benefits size often confers of a perception of power and executive rewards. Rarely do acquisitions add shareholder value.

Bigger is often thought of as better. The management writer, Professor Charles Handy, however, in his book, *The Second Curve*, asks the important question, 'Better for whom?' 'The suspicion must be that it is ego-driven from the top.' 'Growth by acquisition is tempting to those egos, but the result can be an oligopoly of a few big businesses dominating a sector of the economy and thwarting effective competition.' 'When governments collude in the creation of these monster companies through their purchasing policies they are aiding and abetting the kind of oligopolies that they should be outlawing.'[7]

Moeller and Brady in 2014 recognised the biases that can adversely affect deals. They refer to runaway deals, which 'occur when the momentum of the deal takes charge and when executives lose objectivity.' From my own deal-making experiences, it is hard to stop a deal after a certain point, particularly when it has become public knowledge.

When a company makes an acquisition, there is great fanfare. The CEO is a conqueror. There are boastful press releases and optimistic claims for the benefits of the deal and the leader's prowess. To admit that the deal was bad or that the due diligence and valuation were wrong has powerful emotional and credibility consequences for those behind the transaction. Most people cannot admit that they were wrong, naive, inept, incompetent, stupid, or dishonest.

As I outlined before, large goodwill values on a balance sheet that may be vastly overstated can make management highly resistant to restate assets to more realistic values and admit they made a mistake.

The House of Commons Report was damning about Carillion's management, 'lacked a coherent strategy beyond removing competitors.' 'Increasingly reckless in the pursuit of growth.' 'Carillion's forays overseas were largely disastrous.' 'A deliberate, naive and hubristic strategy.' 'Weak supply-chain, poor planning, difficulty adapting to local business practices.' It is interesting to contrast these criticisms in the House of Commons Report to the statements by senior management in the annual reports that were upbeat, expansive, and self-congratulatory.

# Dividends

The headline in the Carillion annual report for 2016 stated, '16 years of increasing dividends' and added, 'The board increased the full-year dividend broadly in line with the growth in underlying earnings.' Carillion's final dividend paid in 2016 was £55 million, and from 2009 to 2016, the company had paid out £554 million in dividends. During the same time, pre-tax profits were £594 million.[8] The board boasted in the 2016 accounts, released in March 2017 that, 'the board has increased the dividend in each of the 16 years since the formation of the company in 1999.'

Jonathan Ford in the 28 January 2018 *Financial Times* noted that in the five years from 2011 to 2016 the top two executives, Richard Howson and Richard Adam, increased their bonuses from nothing to more than £1 million a year.

As I mentioned earlier, an important question we should consider is why should dividends always increase? Particularly in a cyclical industry like construction, we would expect profits to swing up and down, and, intuitively, dividends should also vary over time. Looking at Carillion's numbers, both profits and dividends were steady from 2011 to 2016. Dividends are under management's control, and, to some degree, profits can be manipulated despite internationally agreed accounting standards.

Accounting has many grey areas. For example, management can manipulate work-in-progress, pension fund top-ups, and the value of goodwill – particularly important in Carillion's case. What is interesting about Carillion's accounts is that the cash flow figure swings significantly, and cash is the one area that is more difficult for management to fudge. Cash manipulation, however, does have a couple of powerful levers open to management, and Carillion applied them aggressively. They embraced supply chain finance as I explained earlier, resulting in slower payments to suppliers and retaining cash in the business longer. Supply chain finance also had the advantage of being off-balance-sheet funding, so the firm looked to be financially stronger than it was. In addition, Carillion low bid for government private finance initiatives (PFI) projects that had terms ranging from 20 to 35 years. Those major infrastructure contracts were large, long-term, and, importantly, upfront cash flow positive.

Winning a long-term, loss-making bid with good cash flow is a short-sighted business strategy. After the collapse of Carillion, the government dramatically reduced using PFI finance. Many of those long-term PFI contracts are still running, and in 2022, the NHS spent close to half a billion pounds in interest charges on loans. There are 101 NHS trusts that still owe over £50 billion in future unitary payments.

Generally, greater volatility is seen as indicating greater risk; and the opposite, low volatility, as lower risk, but that is not necessarily true. For example, a Member of Parliament can have a steady income until he loses an election versus a self-employed window cleaner whose income might vary by season and weather.

Steady, stable dividends indicate to the market that the business is steady and stable and implies low risk, and that was certainly the impression the directors wanted the market to have of Carillion's business. We can only speculate what would have been the effect of a different dividend policy. If half of the £554 million paid out from 2009 to 2016 had been retained in the company, would Carillion have survived? Or would the £990 million pension deficit have sunk them anyway? We will never know.

## Market Capitalisation and Profit Warnings

Up to the first quarter of 2016, Carillion's market capitalisation was around £1.2 billion. In March 2017, the company reported flat pre-tax profits and the market capitalisation had drifted down to £1 billion. In May, Richard Howson, the chief executive, stated that there had been 'an encouraging start to the year.' However, on 10 June 2017 the company announced a write down on contracts of £845 million, a fall in cash flow and revenues, the suspension of the dividends, and the resignation of Howson. The market capitalisation collapsed to just over £200 million. More bad news was to follow. On 29 September 2017, further provisions were made for £200 million. The third profit warning in five months was announced on 17 November warning of a breach of debt covenants. By this time, the market capitalisation had fallen by 90 percent and bankruptcy was less than two months away. A public company that had been worth £1.2 billion in January 2016 was worthless within twenty-four months.

When you look carefully at the annual report and accounts, usually running to over 180 pages of statements and disclosures, it seems remarkable that the Carillion management and their auditors so underestimated the scale of their problems and the fragility of the company.

We looked earlier at the Rational Economic Model based on the efficient market hypothesis (EMH). The EMH is the theory that a share price reflects all information and that beating the market with the consistent skills of an investment manager is impossible. It is assumed that shares generally trade at fair value. If the information available to investors is wrong, then the share price, which is in effect what investors think the business is worth, will also be wrong. Why didn't Carillion's share price reflect the true value of the company? Was it because the information was wrong, or did the situation change beyond anyone's reasonable expectations?

How did behavioural factors impact the board's decisions and Carillion's strategy? What effect did the strategy have on the share price and the perception of value and risk in the business? We will examine these questions as we progress through our analysis.

In 2013, Eugene Fama shared the Nobel Prize for economics with Robert Schiller. Their work looked to refute the EMH. Fama and Schiller's essential insight was that publicly available information is incorporated into a security's price. Fama said, 'It is a mistake to think the hypothesis is true or false.' 'Most public information is in the price but not always perfectly. It is a mistake to think that EMH describes the world as it is.' It is a model that is illuminating without being true. Professor Joseph Stigliz of Columbia University, a highly respected American economist, wrote, 'If the EMH was true why would anyone invest in obtaining information in the first place?'

## Cabinet Office Evaluation of Risk

The collapse of Carillion plc in January 2018 raised significant concerns about the government's relationship with and management of its major suppliers and the potential impact on the delivery of important public services.

Carillion had extensive relationships with seventeen government departments and undertook hundreds of public contracts. The company was designated a National Strategic Supplier. Companies that undertake more than £100 million a year in government contracts, effectively being paid with taxpayers money, are monitored by a group at the Cabinet Office. In 2018, there were twenty-eight companies in that category. In July 2017, shortly after announcing their first major profit warning, Carillion was awarded a massive £1.4 billion contract for work on HS2, the planned high-speed rail link from London to Birmingham. HS2 involves many departments and government agencies and was promoted as a national flagship project.

The Cabinet Office uses a traffic light designation to rank risk. Red indicates material concerns and high risk. Amber means material concerns across one or more contracts, and green indicates no known issues. There is a fourth level, black status, that indicates very high risk and is rarely used. The high-risk red warning means serious and persistent underperformance and financial distress.

Following the 10 July 2017 profit warning, Carillion's Amber status, which it had held for several months, was raised to Red. In November 2017, the Cabinet Office recommended a provisional high-risk rating but, following representation from the company, that was not confirmed.

On 28 November 2017, the Government's Chief Commercial Officer sent a formal letter to the CEO, Keith Cochrane, who had taken over from Richard Howson, and the letter advised Carillion that they might be moved to high-risk and that they had until December to respond. It was not until the beginning of January 2018 that a government internal report summarised the fragility of the situation and its near-imminent collapse.

A few days before the Stock Exchange announcement of Carillion's collapse, Jack Simpson reported that the Whitehall Crown Representative responsible for monitoring Carillion, Julie Scattergood, a former Rolls-Royce director of operations, had left the post sometime after May 2017. It appears that there may have been no one in charge of the account when the company announced its half-year loss of £1.15 billion and a major shake-up of its executive team.[9] The Civil Service chief executive and Cabinet Office permanent secretary, Sir John Manzoni, admitted that the key Whitehall link to the company, the Crown Commercial Representative, had been vacant between August and November 2017, a key period in the firm's fall.[10] Why did the government monitoring system fail to capture Carillion's risk level?

## Profit Warning

Investors do not like unpleasant surprises, and a significant unanticipated profit warning undermines confidence in management and manifests itself in a falling share price. On 10 July 2017, Carillion issued the first shocking profit warning. Richard Howson, the CEO, resigned. The shares of Carillion dropped in value by 59 percent, borrowing increased to £961 million, and goodwill – an asset on the balance sheet – was reduced by £134 million.

An important measure of liquidity is the working capital ratio. It is the ratio of current assets to current liabilities, and a ratio of less than 1 is a strong indicator of liquidity problems. After the profit warning and adjustments, Carillion's ratio fell to 0.74. The profit warning conceded that the provision of £729 million of expected revenue that Carillion had previously recognised would not be obtainable.

Tim Steer wrote,

> The collapse in January 2018 of Carillion, which had received enormous amounts of public money as one of the UK government's favourite construction and support services companies, is just one in a long line of corporate disasters where even a cursory look at the balance sheet by anyone with a smattering of financial training would have evoked a feeling of déjà vu and the realization that the company was heading for a fall.

Carillion experienced a very sharp deterioration in the quality of its current assets, leading to a precipitous decline in the share price.

Steer went on to point out that,

> There was a great deal of information in the report and accounts. For example, the amounts owed on construction contracts increased from £387m to £614m, a 46 percent increase. Sales showed virtually no growth over five years. Customers showed signs of slower payment."

The failings of Carillion's management clearly show that if you are not paying attention to the facts, wilfully ignoring them, or in denial, your strategic decisions are going to be flawed. In Carillion's case, fatally.

Carillion was not alone in having problems with huge amounts of goodwill on its balance sheet that turned out to be more like bad will. Thomas Cook, the travel group, went into receivership on 23 September 2019 and offers a similar example to Carillion. Thomas Cook had been in business for 178 years and, when it collapsed, left 150,000 customers stranded abroad. In the end, Thomas Cook was unable to secure a £200 million lifeline that it claimed was all that was needed to keep it going. Like Carillion, the collapse of Thomas Cook can be traced back to a disastrous merger more than ten years earlier. The merger in 2007 with MyTravel was orchestrated by Manny Fontenla-Novoa, who was the CEO. At the time of the collapse, Thomas

Cook's debt reached £1.2 billion, and its goodwill was £1.1 billion. In the end, the MyTravel deal was written off, creating a £1.5 billion loss. Accounting regulators were concerned by the company's use of goodwill, and executives were accused of being too optimistic in their accounting of goodwill. The auditors for Thomas Cook were Ernst and Young. The accountants managing the liquidation charged over £11 million in fees.

Both Carillion and Thomas Cook show that the collapse of a company is often caused by antecedents that go back a long way rather than recent incidents.

## Who Knew and Who Was Shorting the Stock

The Carillion story has come under extensive public and government scrutiny; however, the commentary is blessed with hindsight. It is easy to be wise after an event. Let's consider why a small number of investors understood the dangers and started selling shares twelve to twenty-four months before the collapse. Why did most shareholders stay invested?

At the time of Carillion's collapse, banks and brokers were cutting back on funding research. New financial services regulations called MiFID 2 resulted in an unbundling of charges, making it difficult for stockbrokers to charge clients for research. Analysts were spread thin, resulting in them covering too many stocks and not having enough time or resources to undertake deep analysis. Before the collapse, three-quarters of analysts had a hold rating on Carillion's stock, and the market consensus was hold. With so much information contained in the over 180-page annual report and accounts, it is perhaps challenging to make a buy/sell/hold recommendation, and hold is the safe setting. Contrarian thinking is always challenging and risky. Analysts need to be well versed in business management and financial accounting skills. In addition, they need enough time to properly analyse a company, speak to the management, and be confident to make tough judgement calls.

One major Carillion investor, Standard Life Aberdeen, began to gradually divest in December 2015 owing to concerns about financial management, strategy, and corporate governance. Standard Life held biannual meetings with Carillion's board from 2014, and concerns were raised about the widening pension deficit, high levels of debt, weak cash generation, and an unwillingness of the board to change strategic direction. One of the last meetings with the CEO was on 17 July 2017, by which time Standard Life's shareholding was minimal. They disposed of all their shares by the end of 2017.[12]

In 2017, Carillion was one of the most shorted stocks on the Stock Exchange. Short selling is a technique that traders use to profit if the value of a company's shares decline, basically a bet that the current share price is overvalued. It is a high-risk, high-reward strategy, generating exponential returns if the bet is correct but significant losses if the trader is wrong about the direction of the stock price or the time it will take for the stock to fall. Short selling was a clear warning sign of market concerns about Carillion's performance.

By 2017, another indicator of serious problems was the inability of suppliers to buy credit insurance on Carillion. It appears that the credit insurance industry was aware of the risks ahead of many investors.

Reflecting on the performance of analysts, could more scrutiny of the Carillion accounts have highlighted the problems earlier? Should analysts have been able to spot the weaknesses? Should higher-than-industry-average margins raise warning flags? Should there have been more sensitivity analysis of the high levels of goodwill and the sensitivity of pension liabilities to small changes in discount rates and inflation? Would analysis using behavioural finance techniques have highlighted the risks earlier? Why did short selling not have a greater impact on share price and risk assessment? When we examine human biases, we will discover plausible explanations for why most investors ignored the warning signs.

## The Pension Deficit

Carillion acquired two large, established companies: Mowlem in 2006 and Alfred McAlpine in 2008. Both businesses had significant pension liabilities for former and future retirees. By the time of Carillion's collapse, their pension obligations covered 27,000 people.

Not all pension liabilities are the same. The riskiest were the defined-benefit pensions. Defined-benefit pensions pay out based on past earnings rather than past contributions. These defined benefit payments are normally inflation protected, so that payments ten, twenty, or thirty years after an employee has retired can be enormous and can easily exceed an employee's salary during their time with a firm.

Under the 2004 UK Pensions Act, schemes need to compute a 'technical valuation of their liabilities to ensure that they have adequate funds in the pension pot to meet expected pay-outs. Pension calculations use a discounted cash flow taking account of projected prices, earnings, and investment returns over the life of the pension. Trustees must take steps to eliminate any deficit.' The challenge is that it is impossible to accurately predict these future valuations, and small variations in expected rates of inflation or investment value growth have a greatly amplified impact on the surplus or shortfall of assets to meet the pension liabilities.

Naturally, companies want to minimise the money that they put in their pension funds, as it is then unavailable for investment in the business or to pay a dividend to shareholders. Pension calculations are complex and carried out by experts called actuaries who apply mathematical, accounting, statistical, and analytical principles to establish estimates of life expectancy and to estimate how much a pension fund needs to hold to meet its future liabilities. Actuaries analyse risk to measure the probability of future events.

The House of Commons report highlighted the point that 'Funding pension schemes is an obligation. Paying dividends is not.' The big issue that nobody wanted to talk about at Carillion was the rapidly increasing pension deficit. In 2016, the pension liability was £3.4 billion – three times the company's 2016 market capitalisation – with pension assets of £2.6bn. That was a pension deficit in 2016 of £895 million.

For many quoted companies, focusing on dividends rather than addressing pension fund deficits was not uncommon. Companies in the UK FTSE 350 Index paid seven times more cash to shareholders in 2017 on a combined basis than they did in plugging their pension scheme deficits. They paid £8.7 billion in pension-deficit contributions in 2017 and £66 billion in dividends. At the same time, the Pensions Regulator faced increased pressure to force companies to clear the deficits in their defined benefit pension schemes more quickly.

FTSE 350 companies made average pension contributions of around 10 percent of dividends in 2016 and 2017 and ended 2017 with their retirement funds in a healthier state, largely due to stronger stock market conditions. At the end of 2017, the combined pension deficits for FTSE 350 companies were £55bn, down from £62 billion in 2016. By June 2018, this had been reduced to £35 billion because of better stock market conditions.[13] By September 2021, according to pensions firm, Mercer, the FTSE 350 combined pension deficit had risen to between £82 billion and £103 billion but fell to £45 billion by May 2022. As you can see, small changes in interest rates and the value of equities have a significant effect on the scale of pension liabilities.[14]

As Kay and King note,

> The requirement to make plans to eliminate the deficit shown by the technical valuation, enforced by the pension regulator, was introduced to ensure that if the scheme was to close, there would be sufficient funds to guarantee the pension promise. Laudable at first, the system risks bankrupting firms if they are unable to meet their liabilities. The regulatory regime is trying to reduce risks for the pension recipients. However, the requirements may well have increased the risks to pension recipients.[15]

Ultimately, pensioners are protected by various government guarantee schemes. However, we must not forget that the collapse of Carillion directly affected over 40,000 employees, shareholders, customers, and tens of thousands of small firms – and the significant cost to taxpayers has never been properly assessed or disclosed. What can't be priced is the broader reputational damage to large companies and their directors, to business in general, and to the credibility of large accounting firms and city financiers.

## Carillion Board, Corporate Governance, and Executive Responsibility

### The Role of the Board of Directors

I want to look more closely at the board, the personalities, and their backgrounds, and to summarise the obligations of those who run our largest companies. It is quite wrong to imagine that companies and directors are free to make decisions as they please. There is a vast range of legal obligations and codes that define and prescribe how those who run companies must behave.

The Companies Act 2006 is the single longest piece of legislation passed by Parliament, and in 742 densely typed pages, it contains 1,300 sections and 16 schedules. The Act contains extensive provisions regarding the behaviour of directors.

There is also the UK Corporate Governance Code, also known as the Combined Code, which is part of UK company law and sets out the principles of good corporate governance. It is maintained by the Financial Reporting Council and applies to all listed companies. The Code states that the key purpose of the board 'is to ensure the company's prosperity by collectively directing the company's affairs whilst meeting the appropriate interests of its shareholders and stakeholders.' It has five sections: Leadership, Effectiveness, Accountability, Remuneration, and Relations with Shareholders. We will examine these responsibilities as we look at the behaviour of the board and consider how well Carillion's directors met those obligations?

**Leadership:** Every company should be headed by an effective board that is collectively responsible for the long-term success of the company. The chairman is responsible for the leadership of the board. The CEO is responsible for the running of the company's business. The role of non-executive directors is to constructively challenge and help develop proposals on strategy.

**Effectiveness:** The board and its committees should have an appropriate balance of skills, experience, and independence.

**Accountability:** The board is responsible for maintaining sound risk management and internal control systems and should be formal and transparent.

**Remuneration:** Sufficient to attract, retain, and motivate directors with the quality required. A significant proportion of remuneration should be related to performance.

**Relations with shareholders:** Dialogue should be based on a mutual understanding of objectives.

The Governance Code also offers guidelines on board composition for larger public companies like Carillion. A board should have around twelve members, the majority of whom should be non-executive directors (NEDs). Each board must also appoint a senior independent director as well as chairmen for audit, remuneration, and nomination committees. It is typical to have the CEO and CFO as executive directors and perhaps one additional senior executive.

In 2012, the London Stock Exchange (LSE) first published official guidance on corporate governance for firms listed on the UK's main stock market, and it generally follows the Corporate Governance Code. In the old days, matters were handled through discrete calls to senior directors. According to Alastair Walmsley, Head of Primary Markets, 'High standards of corporate governance make an important contribution to companies' long-term performance.'

Whether it is realistic or not, directors of UK companies in general, and most specifically directors of publicly listed companies, are legally obliged to be familiar with these acts and codes. We have many questions to consider about the performance and behaviour of Carillion's directors. The top of the pyramid was small as there were only two executive board members, and there were doubts about their competence. Although the salaries appeared relatively high, were they too low to attract top players to manage a complex international business? Was the lack of strong NEDs a contributory factor in the collapse, or is there a broader problem with the way many boards function?

What happens when personal goals conflict with organisational goals, and which groups of stakeholders should have priority in conflicts of interests? Do incentive schemes encourage behaviour that is incompatible with good corporate governance? These and other issues will be explored in this section.

## Richard Howson, Carillion CEO 2012–2017

Let's now look at the senior leadership team at Carillion. Richard Howson became the CEO of the group in January 2012, when he was forty-three years old. He was eventually dismissed in July 2017. Howson worked at Tarmac before the foundation of Carillion in 1999 when it demerged from Tarmac and spent twenty-five years with the two companies, more than half his career. He moved from his role managing Carillion's interests in the Middle East to become the Chief Operating Officer in 2010 and, by all accounts, was a solid and competent construction engineer. In 2016, his base salary was £660,000 and part of a package worth £1.5 million, which was not especially high for equivalent positions in large, complex public companies. When asked by the select committee why the Carillion chief executive's salary was increased by 50 percent over the two years before the collapse, the chair of the firm's remuneration committee said that it had been 'benchmarked' and that 'it was Carillion's policy to pay median.'

I have spoken with several senior people who knew Howson well, and they universally described him as a good and decent man who was trying to do his best. Richard Howson must have been under enormous pressure towards the end of his time at Carillion and was probably in over his head. He inherited problems going back years before his appointment to the board. At the time of taking over as CEO, there was only one full-time colleague on the group board, CFO Richard Adam.

Examining how the senior directors made decisions from a behavioural perspective brings fresh insight into what went wrong at Carillion. We all exhibit biases in our thinking and decision-making, and these biases are strengthened when we are under stress, afraid, threatened, and in times of crisis. Stress changes our behaviour. We become more angry, irritable, and defensive; rational communication becomes more difficult; and we act more impulsively.

Sir Ronald Wingate, who headed the oddly-named London Controlling Section during the Second World War, a group dedicated to military deception, explained how worries are magnified when you lose the initiative. 'One who has lost the sense of being in control is more likely to take council of his fears.' Did Howson's fears for Carillion take control of his decision-making, and if so, did that start months before the July 2017 dramatic profit warning, or was the fear growing years earlier?

It's worth remembering as we examine this case study based on analysis of the accounts, detailed annual reports, and press commentary that all organisations are run by people with hopes, fears, stresses, a private and public persona, family and personal issues, and all of the personal and human psychology that each of us deals with.

It is also important to understand that a chief executive cannot be far out of line with the current market expectations of their company. The prevailing mood of the market punishes leaders who have a contrarian view. And voters and shareholders prefer leaders who peddle dreams. Even if Richard Howson had been aware of the gravity of the situation years before the collapse and wanted to take robust action by, for example, reducing the dividend programme and conserving cash, would the board have agreed, or would the market have accepted the strategy?

The House of Commons committee said, 'Mr. Howson demonstrated little grasp of the unsustainability of Carillion's business model or the basic failings of governance that lay at the root of its problems.' Howson opened his evidence by stating that 'but for a few very challenging contracts, predominantly in the Oman and one in Qatar, I believe Carillion would have survived.'[16] He even seemed surprised to have been removed as Chief Executive following the profit warning, arguing 'the business was in a sustainable position' based on the support it was receiving from banks.

In Howson's world, Carillion was a healthy business that fell victim to a series of unforeseeable events over which it had no control. In fact, Mr. Howson had a responsibility to ensure he was well informed about performance and risk and to act on areas of weakness. Rather than make the fundamental changes needed, he spent much of his time chasing down the consequences of the company's mistakes. His misguided self-assurance obscured an apparent lack of interest in, or understanding of, essential detail or any recognition that Carillion was a business crying out for change and reform.

The House of Commons committee described Howson as a 'Figurehead for a business that careened progressively out of control . . . misguidedly self-assured leadership.' And added, 'The individuals who failed in their responsibilities in running Carillion and in challenging, advising or regulating it, were often acting entirely in line with their personal incentives.'

The House of Commons committee, of course, viewed events after the outcome was known. As the saying goes, it is easy to be wise after the event. A common behavioural bias is the 'Fundamental Attribution Error.' We view the errors of other people because of their personal flaws, but we view our own errors as a result of external factors.

## Richard Adam, Carillion CFO 2007–2016

Richard Adam was fifty years old when he became Carillion's Finance Director in 2007, and he held the top financial job for ten years. Adam retired in 2016. During his time as the group's most senior financial officer, Carillion completed its largest acquisitions including Alfred McAlpine, Eaga, and the aborted Balfour Beatty merger. He was directly involved in all the key executive decisions at the highest level including bank funding, new finance initiatives, acceptance of key contracts, and pension deficit funding.

The House of Commons investigation described Richard Adam as the 'Architect of aggressive accounting policies' at Carillion, and as the senior director who 'refused to make adequate contributions to . . . pension schemes.' Adam claimed that Carillion's dividend policy was 'balancing the needs of many stakeholders including pensioners, staff, and shareholders.'

An American legal case, United States versus Jewell, that involved the transportation of illegal drugs, defined 'wilful blindness' or 'wilful ignorance' as a person intentionally keeping themselves unaware of the facts, and it was ruled that wilful blindness would still render them liable or implicated. Wilful blindness is a legal term that has now come to mean any situation where someone intentionally turns their attention away from an ethical or legal problem.

In 2016, his final year, Adam's salary package was £1.1 million, plus an employer pension contribution of £163,000. At the first available opportunity, Adam sold all his shares, which were worth £776,000 on 1 March 2017. The House of Commons said that was 'the actions of a man who knew where the company was heading.' A week later, on 8 May 2017, Adam's long-term incentive plan awards for 2014 vested, and he sold the total amount of shares for £242,000.

Because senior managers and directors have inside information, they are restricted in when they can buy and sell shares in their own companies. So the window of opportunity for Adam to liquidate his share options in Carillion during his time as finance director will have been restricted. However, assuming Adam no longer had access to relevant inside information following retirement, he was acting legally in selling his shares, although it doesn't necessarily inspire confidence when the ex-finance director bails. The action, in view of what happened, does raise questions about how much Adam knew about the vulnerability of the company, the impact of creative accounting, and how fragile the business was. Adam clearly benefited from a strong share price, and any strategy that, for example, reduced dividends to increase cash would have most likely had an impact on the share price and, hence, the value of his share options and eventual personal net worth.

Behavioural psychology may be able to give some insight into Adam's behaviour. According to the psychologist and writer Dan Ariely, it is a 'lot easier to cheat and not feel bad about it when using non-monetised elements, for example, tokens or share options. Breaking the link with cash releases people from feeling bad. We rationalise dishonesty with non-monetary items; it is easier to justify our behaviour to ourselves. Non-monetary currencies can lead us astray. As a simple example, most people wouldn't think of stealing £10 from petty cash but might happily help themselves to some pens and stationery from the office.[17]

Carillion's senior management may not have stolen cash, but grabbing some tokens of stock options appears to have been acceptable.

## Philip Green, Carillion Chairman 2014–2018

Philip Neville Green is a British business executive born in 1953. He was chairman of the board of Carillion from 2014 until its final liquidation in January 2018. He was also the chairman of Baker Corp., a rental equipment business, from 2011 to 2017. His earlier career included five years as the managing director of the home furnishing division of the Coloroll Group, and he was the group managing director from 1989 to 1990.

In 1994, as a trustee of the Coloroll Group's pension fund, Green was found guilty of a breach of trust and maladministration of the scheme by the Pensions Ombudsman, a fact that resonates with what happened at Carillion. Other jobs included a senior role at DHL, four years with Thomson Reuters, and then CEO of Royal P&O Nedlloyd from 2003 to 2006. Green was CEO of United Utilities plc, the United Kingdom's largest listed water company founded in 1995 after the merger of North West Water and NORWEB, and it was a major electricity distributor in the North West until 2010. Green joined the Carillion board in 2011 as a senior non-executive director initially and as chairman in 2014.[18]

Philip Green should not be confused with Sir Philip Green of Arcadia and Top Shop fame, who is coincidentally just a few months younger. Carillion's Green was active in Conservative political circles, a friend of David Cameron, and the recipient of a CBE in the 2014 Honours List.

The UK Corporate Governance Code says that a company's chairman is 'responsible for leadership of the board and ensuring its effectiveness on all aspects of its role.' The code states that the key requirements are: (1) run the board as an effective team; (2) oversee the process of strategy development; (3) be accessible to the CEO and executive team for support and counsel; (4) complement the CEO in shareholder relationships; (5) ensure succession processes; (6) clear and effective communication at all levels; and (7) devote 1–3 days per week to the role. In addition, a listed company chairman should have prior experience, a successful track record, and be well respected.

Whilst the chairman supports the CEO, he also has a responsibility to make sure that the CEO operates within acceptable guidelines and does not go unchallenged on important issues or run through board matters without proper examination.

In his position as chairman, Philip Green oversaw low levels of investment, declining cash flow, rising debt, and a growing pension deficit. Yet his board agreed to year-on-year dividend increases and a rise in remuneration for his executive board colleagues from £1.8 million to £3.0 million.[19] Mr. Green was still at the helm when the company crashed in January 2018.

One serious problem for Carillion was that Philip Green did not understand the complex construction sector. The House of Commons report was scathing about him, 'He interpreted his role as to be an unquestioning optimist, an outlook he maintained in a delusional, upbeat assessment of the company's prospects only days before it began its public decline.' 'Carillion's board are both responsible and culpable for the company's failure. They presented to us as self-pitying victims.' 'But the problems . . . were long in the making as, too, was the rotten corporate culture.' 'Carillion's rise and spectacular fall was a story of recklessness, hubris, and greed. Its business model was a relentless dash for cash driven by acquisitions, rising debt, expansion into new markets, and exploitation of suppliers.'

From a behavioural perspective, we can highlight several common biases: optimism bias, overestimating the probabilities of positive things, and underestimating the probability of risks. It should be noted that the opposite, pessimism bias, can be equally risky. And we can speculate that during board meetings there were probably several other cognitive biases at work including: confirmation bias, where we tend to listen to and hear information that confirms our preconceptions; the bandwagon effect, a powerful form of group think; the well-known ostrich effect, where we ignore dangerous or negative information; and selective perception, where we allow our expectations to influence what we perceive.

The House of Commons report was damning, but how fair is it to describe Carillion as having a 'rotten culture?' Perhaps it is fairer to say that the two executive directors had a toxic culture that permeated the business, at least in later years, and they were in denial about the gravity and precariousness of the company. Certainly, by any measure, Philip Green failed abysmally as chairman.

## Keith Cochrane, Interim CEO July 2017

Following the dramatic profit warning and restatement of the company's accounts, Richard Howson was replaced by Keith Cochrane. In July 2015,

Cochrane was appointed as the senior independent non-executive director, a role that Philip Green had held from 2011 to 2014. In July 2017, following the massive profit warning, Cochrane was appointed interim CEO with a fee package of £750,000.

Cochrane's background was at Weir Group plc, a Scottish multinational engineering business with 15,000 employees. He was the Group Finance Director from 2006, becoming Group Chief Executive in 2009. Cochrane retired as a director of Weir in 2016. According to an insider, he didn't understand the construction sector; however, he did have experience running a large and complex company and was a qualified accountant who had trained with Arthur Andersen.

The House of Commons commented that Cochrane gave, 'Limited and vague responses to fairly fundamental questions about Carillion and had only a vague grasp of finances' (Times 19 February 18). He described net debt and the pension deficit as 'lesser concerns' in 2015. The committee added, 'He came with extensive board-level experience, yet quickly succumbed to the dysfunctionality prevalent on the board,' and they were 'unimpressed by his inability to offer "any meaningful information" about how the company proposed to address its financial problems, or "give answers . . . considered satisfactory to relatively straightforward questions." '[20] In January 2021, the Insolvency Service sought to ban Cochrane and seven former Carillion directors from holding senior boardroom positions.

There was probably little or nothing that Cochrane could have done to turn around Carillion. The slow death of the company started many years earlier. The top of the Carillion pyramid was small with only two executive board members who were supported by a group of non-executive directors with limited time to get to the bottom of serious structural problems that were well hidden by creative and/or false accounting.

## The Consultant's Report, Strategic Issues, and Risk for Carillion

Let's now look at strategic issues at Carillion and review concepts of risk. In late 2017, Ernst & Young (EY) was engaged to undertake a strategic review. EY is a multinational professional services firm headquartered in London. They have over 300,000 employees and are considered one of the Big Four global accounting firms. Their strategy report was presented between December 2017 and early January 2018, just weeks before Carillion's collapse.

The EY consultants delivered a detailed 100-page top-level review of Carillion's business with a clear strategic plan. We are going to spend time going through the report because it highlights important corporate strategy issues that Carillion had largely failed to address, and where they had dealt with issues, the implementation achieved no demonstrable effect.

EY were paid fees of £10.8 million for six months of work that turned out to be of no value to anyone. It is unusual to have access to this level of confidential detail, and the report gives us a fascinating insight into external advice delivered to the directors. But, of course, it was too late. The patient was a corpse.

The EY report found a 'lack of professionalism and expertise' and a 'lack of accountability' which, it observed, 'prioritized short-term benefits over sustainable performance.'[21] The Internal Strategy report said, 'In response to significant contract losses and provisions, the group has implemented structural change. It is taking action to improve the quality of senior management and is enhancing the risk management framework.'

An important question is why Carillion's leadership had not effectively addressed important issues over the previous ten years. Or were they aware of them but couldn't face the impact of correcting the situation?

Following the consultant's recommendations, Carillion announced, 'The Board will be bolstered through four new appointments including a new CEO,' and added, 'The current focus is on short-term business-critical actions, and a new CFO and new COO will be appointed from within the Group.' Surprisingly the consultants made no mention of replacing Philip Green, who would continue as chairman. Keith Cochrane, the interim CEO, was to step down in 2018. Andrew Davies, the former CEO of Wates Group, a large private construction group where he had done a turnaround, was to be the new CEO.

One of the Non-Executives of Carillion, Baroness Sally Morgan, who had become the Senior Independent Director, was the former Director of Government Relations in Downing Street from 2001–2005. She was appointed in July 2017 and served on the audit, business integrity, nomination, renumeration, and sustainability committees. She retired in January 2018.[22]

The EY consultants proposed new NEDs, including the well-respected Alan Lovell, who was Chairman of the Consumer Council for Water and an NED at Flowgroup plc. Lovell was the former CEO of Infinis, Costain, and Jarvis. The consultants, no doubt under pressure from the banks, proposed a major clear-out of the remaining leadership team, but it was all too late.

The EY Report, published in early January 2018, gave a snapshot of Carillion's key problems – and the comments were damning. It is interesting to reflect on how different the consultant's picture of the business is compared with the upbeat public image presented in annual reports.

The Ernst & Young consultants identified numerous problems including that contracts were too complex, there were too many layers of management, there was too much focus on the short term, and 'noisy data' prevented management from seeing the scale of the problems clearly. Carillion suffered from 'not very busy' overhead combined with many unprofitable contracts.

The consultants pointed out that profits relied on one-offs such as the disposal of Private Finance Initiative (PFI) contracts and that mobilisation costs on new projects were too high, combined with too much bidding on unprofitable contracts with negative cash flow. They noted the lack of accountability and professionalism, the lack of a common bid process, that Carillion was 'constantly reinventing the wheel,' and that contract execution was heavily dependent on third parties with poor management of customer claims and unrealistic timescales.

The EY report highlighted insufficient rigour, a lack of joined-up leadership, and poor planning. If that wasn't enough, they cited a lack of robust supplier management, group and divisional leadership's lack of problem ownership, and contract requirements ignored combined with a lack of clear management. 'The Group had become too complex with an overly short-term focus, weak operational risk management, with too many distractions outside the core business. It adds up to a condemning list of incompetence and failure.'[23] These were serious charges of mismanagement, incompetence, dereliction of duty, and failure. The difference between the company's bullish public face and what the consultants were seeing was dramatic, painting a completely different picture from the press releases and published accounts.

On a positive note, the consultant's report stated that Carillion had great strengths with a strong brand, a leading market position, deep customer relationships, and a broad customer base. They highlighted the 43,000 skilled workforce, an order book of £12.9 billion, plus a new business pipeline of £28.8 billion. The order book looks impressive, representing more than two years of business, but we will never know if these were profitable projects.

How did the company get this far when these problems were clearly there for years and getting worse over time? Is the Carillion case an example of how much damage two executives and a dysfunctional board can do to a large, listed company? But what about the roles of the auditors, consultants, bankers, and investment analysts? Perhaps the consultant's report was two, three, or even five to ten years too late. It is fair to say that Carillion's leaders displayed 'ostrich management.' Their heads were in the sand; they were hoping danger would go away, and scope neglect existed, which, in simple terms, means ignoring the size of a problem.

Let's look at Carillion's Vision Statement taken from the last annual report in 2016. 'Our vision is to be the trusted partner for providing services, delivering infrastructure, and creating places that bring lasting benefits to our customers and the communities in which we live and work.'

In the front of the same annual report, the company's stated values were, 'We care, we achieve together, we improve, we deliver. Our values shape the way we do business, how we work with each other, our customers, our suppliers, our partners, and all those with whom we interact when delivering our services.'

In hindsight, these vacuous statements were meaningless promises. Values and vision need to be sincere and have true buy-in from all senior executives across the business. Clearly, this was not the case at the top of the organisation at Carillion.

Looking to the future, EY consultants recommended Carillion focus on the right clients for repeat business and cross-selling opportunities. They said that Carillion should do fewer things better, a tag line the consultants took from a senior executive in the company, Carillion should reduce distractions, improve the certainty of delivery, and concentrate on their core activities by exiting non-core activities. They should improve their business terms and use the right people. This is sadly typical of the recommendations consultants churn out in their reports to executives who should have been on top of these things for years and were well paid for doing just that.

When consultants are paid £750 an hour and they submit a £10 million report advising public company directors that they need to focus on the 'right' clients, you have to reflect on the ability of Carillion's leadership – and the value of the consultants! Surprisingly, the 100-page consultant report does not mention the pension deficit – a major factor in Carillion's demise.

Reading the EY report, you would think that the issues raised were matters that the management should have been addressing for a decade. The report is textbook business school/consultant material that could have been written by most MBAs. For Carillion, the report came too late. The challenge facing advisers is that if senior executives are not listening, not interested, or not able to face business challenges, then no consultant is going to fix the mess.

Ironically, EY suggested appointing a new head of risk, an external appointment to be made in Q1 2018, and a move unlikely to have had any short-term impact considering the scale of Carillion's problems. In fact, Carillion had a head of risk for many years. Had the former executives still been in charge, that suggestion would probably have been ignored. A former high-level executive told me that these recommendations were the stated focus areas for years, suggesting that nothing would have changed without leadership/regime change. He claimed that the real reasons for failure were poor strategic decisions linked to the questionable quality of leadership. For example, the decision to undertake large contracts in Qatar without a trusted local partner was naive and, perhaps more serious, acquisitions had been reckless.

Carillion had an overriding short-term focus that drove many business decisions; for example, breaking good governance guidelines for short-term benefits such as taking on high-risk Public Finance Initiative (PFI) contracts. PFI allows the government to access private sector finance to fund large infrastructure projects and often provides the supplier with significant positive cash flow in the short term, but it comes with long-term delivery liabilities and costs. Other poor decisions include failing to dispose of non-core assets, undertaking aggressive trading to support dividend payments, and, of course, failing to address the increasing pension deficit.

In summary, Carillion's business became too complex for the ability of its management. With 326 subsidiaries, too many distractions outside the core of a complex business, and weak financial information at project level, Carillion was overseen by a small, arrogant executive board that was unwilling to recognise the gravity of the situation until it was too late. The company did have a good grasp of the details of the business but fatally lacked the leadership capabilities to take on the big strategic challenges.

We must pose the question of are there many more large companies in similar positions to Carillion? On a much smaller scale, NMCN plc went into administration in October 2021 after it failed to secure new financing. That construction company had 1,700 employees and was founded in 1946 as North Midland Construction. In June 2021, the directors agreed to a £24 million refinancing proposal, selling control to a group of new investors. Unfortunately, the 2020 accounts could not be signed off, and that was a condition of the new funding. Losses for 2020 were expected to be £43 million. Trading was suspended in June 2021, and shareholders have lost all of their funds. Just a year earlier, in 2019, NMCN published its results, showing double-digit growth in revenue and profits with a pre-tax profit of £7.4 million on turnover of £404 million and £26 million in cash in the bank.

The collapse of NMCN had nothing to do with COVID or supply shortages. We must look back to the collapse of Carillion in January 2018 and the tightening accounting rules that followed. No longer could anticipated revenue be accounted for as money banked. There was a warning of trouble ahead in the summer of 2020 when Dan Taylor, the finance director for seven years, was moved out and, shortly after, the CEO departed. In September 2020, the group indicated that losses for the year would be around £15 million. Two major water projects worth £160 million contributed to the problems. A new finance director and CEO were recruited as the losses kept increasing to an estimated £23 million by May 2021. By August 2021, the estimated losses were £43 million, and accounts were further delayed.

Although a publicly quoted company, 48 percent of the shares of NMCN were owned by the founding Moyle family. True, NMCN plc was small in comparison to Carillion, and perhaps the problems that have been highlighted at Carillion were not contributory factors, but the challenges of the construction sector were certainly a factor.[24]

## Notes

1 www.theconstructionindex.co.uk/market-data/top-100-construction-companies/2017.
2 "Defeated," *The Guardian*, August 15, 2014.
3 House of Commons, *Business, Energy and Industrial Strategy and Work and Pensions Committees* (London: House of Commons, May 16, 2019), section 373.
4 *Civil Service World*, February 12, 2018.
5 *The Guardian*, January 14, 2020. Institute for Government.

6  *FT*, May 13, 2020.

7  Charles Handy, *The Second Curve* (London: Random House, 2015), 91.

8  *Construction News*, January 22, 2018.

9  *Construction News*, January 8, 2018, Jack Simpson.

10  *Civil Service World*, February 12, 2018.

11  Tim Steer, *The Signs Were There* (IPS, 2021).

12  HoC 49, 4.96.

13  *FT*, August 3, 2018.

14  uk.mercer.com.

15  John Kay and Mervyn King, *Radical Uncertainty* (New York: W. W. Norton, 2020).

16  HoC 196.

17  Dan Ariely, *Predictably Irrational* (New York: Harper Collins, 2010), 300.

18  https://en.wikipedia.org/wiki/Philip_Nevill_Green.

19  HoC 224.

20  Ibid., 769.

21  *The Telegraph*. Damning EY report reveals widespread cultural problems at Carillion, March 2, 2018. Rhiannon Curry.

22  Jon Robinson, 3 July 2017. Andrew Dougal, the chair of the Audit Committee was to step down in 2018.

23  EY Report presented December 2017–January 2018, 97.

24  www.theconstructionindex.co.uk/news/view/nmcn-what-the-hell-happened.

# 4

# BEHAVIOURAL MANAGEMENT

'Felix, qui potuit rerum cognoscere causas.'

'Fortunate is he who understands the cause of things.'
— Virgil 70 BC–19 BC.

Now that we have explored the history and personalities at Carillion, it is time to examine behavioural thinking and link this to the case history. You will recall that earlier I introduced Herbert Simon, who was awarded a Nobel Prize in 1978 for his work on decision-making. Among his many insights was that humans have limited thinking skills, and he described this as Bounded Rationality and used the word bounded, in the sense of a boundary. He suggested that rational choice theory, the idea that we can and do make rational decisions, is an unrealistic description of the human decision-making process. He observed that we are limited by three things: the information we have, our cognitive limitations, and the finite amount of time available to make a decision.

Daniel Kahneman wrote in 2003,

DOI: 10.4324/9781003457398-5

At the core of behavioural economics is the insight that humans do not behave in line with the assumptions of rationality postulated by standard economic theory. In contrast, humans display bounded rationality, enabling the situational context of an Individual or group to influence their behaviour.[1]

Satisficing, another Simon term, means searching through the alternatives until an acceptable threshold is met. It is how decision-makers actually work. When an optimal decision cannot be determined, we accept a good enough solution.

The theory of Bounded Rationality helps us understand the challenges the Carillion leadership faced. The business was so complex with hundreds of subsidiaries operating across multiple sectors, geographies, and business units together with a mixture of public and private contracts. If the operational dimensions were not enough, there were all the challenges of corporate finance, pension obligations, director compliance, succession management, and city pressure. From this perspective, it is perhaps remarkable that the company managed to survive for so long.

There are many fascinating aspects to behavioural science, and one area that resonates with the Carillion story is how biases affect decision-making. We are going to look in depth at common biases, of which there are a vast number, and we will speculate on how these behavioural factors might have impacted the company's history. The optimism bias, also called the overconfidence bias, is a good example. It is interesting to reflect on when overconfidence becomes delusion, what indications there are that you have crossed the line, and when you know that you are dealing in untruths because of the delusion of your overconfidence.

## Information Bottlenecks

Inside organisations, there is a decision-making process flowing up from across the organisation to the key decision-makers at the top and flowing back to the roots below. Senior managers have limited time to deal with the many complex issues facing their organisation. On top of the ongoing challenges of running a business, urgent incidents demand immediate management focus, and routine tasks that are time consumptive conspire to push long-term strategic issues to the side. If Carillion was in a permanent state of firefighting, how much clear-thinking time could the executive directors realistically spend on strategic issues?

Most large organisations – whether commercial, political, or philanthropic – have a bottleneck at the top of the organisation. Simon states this rather technically, 'the intricacy of chains of consequences are all severely restricted by the limited capacities of the available processors.'[2] The challenge is dealing with an avalanche of information. This is compounded because important information for long-term strategic decisions often originates outside the organisation. As we move up the management hierarchy, the bottleneck gets narrower and narrower, and only a few items can end up at the top of a senior manager's agenda.

Time is a scarce resource at the top of any entity, so it becomes essential to distinguish between problems that have defined timelines and those that are flexible. Bounded Rationality limits the depth and breadth of alternatives that can be considered. There is the added danger that urgent – for example, media-driven – issues rather than important strategic matters dominate the top agenda.

An issue related to bottlenecks is the degree of centralisation versus decentralisation of decision-making. There is a long-running management debate on this structural issue, and the popularity of each approach ebbs and flows every decade, shifting with leadership changes or even management fashion. Bottlenecks cause greater challenges under a centralised control structure. In Carillion's case, the preferred model was for increasingly centralised control that narrowed the bottleneck, and the problem was compounded by a leadership culture that discouraged contrarian thinking. It is perhaps not surprising that Carillion's siege mentality discouraged open debate, avoided facing up to critical issues, and increasingly shifted to top-down diktat.

## The Behavioural Model

The behavioural model considers human behaviour and how it affects decision-making and actions. We try to understand behaviour, observing biases and emotions, and we consider how they affect us and our decision-making dynamics. Behavioural theories of leadership focus on the study of behaviours of leaders.

Our behaviour is governed by reinforcements. When a behaviour is regularly rewarded, it most likely persists. When it is punished, it most likely desists. Understanding what behaviour is being rewarded helps us understand what motivations might be driving a particular set of decisions, and often those motivations are incongruent with the objectives of other stakeholders. By developing our understanding of biases, and examining the motivations of decision-makers, we become attuned to the dangers that biases pose to good decision-making.

In the case of Carillion, it is illuminating to consider how the executive directors were being rewarded both financially and egotistically. We need to consider what behavioural factors might have driven decisions that eventually led to the collapse of the company. Important strategic decisions – for example, the major acquisitions, the increasing dividends policy, or the manipulation of profits – were influenced by behavioural factors that the rational economic model discounts.

We generally think that executives are motivated by money. However, social learning theory proposes that monetary rewards aren't the sole or even the most powerful force behind motivation. Other factors are important such as thoughts, beliefs, morals, feedback, verbal persuasion, job hygiene factors, and recognition – to name a few. Pulling off a large acquisition doesn't just increase a company's market share. It also makes the executives more powerful, raises their profiles, and makes them bigger fish in their pond.

## Case for the Behavioural Model

From a rational economic perspective, human behaviour often appears irrational and sub-optimal, focused on the short term, and subject to biases. But when considered from a behavioural perspective, these behaviours may be quite rational.

Organisational behaviour is often chaotic, unstructured, and dominated by personal agendas. After all, organisations are made up of individuals with their own ambitions and neuroses that may or may not align with the objectives of other stakeholders. We need a broader and more flexible approach to thinking about organisational strategy that is based on real-world dynamics with an understanding of behaviour that leads to poor decision-making.

Cognitive bias is a systematic error in thinking that affects decisions and judgements.[3] Cognitive biases lead us to deviate from rational logic and can result in suboptimal choices and errors. We all have cognitive biases, and we operate with our own personal agendas and pressures. By enhancing our understanding of our own and the biases of others, we are better equipped to navigate the pitfalls of decision-making.

Making important decisions is stressful and time consuming and, unconsciously, we allow our biases to ease the mental strain and pressure. Unfortunately, these biases can take us in the wrong direction. That is to say, a bias can relieve psychological pressure by helping us to avoid the real problems. Strategic thinking is complex. We deal with many known and unknown variables both inside and outside our organisations. Parameters are in constant flux, and pressure comes not just from dealing with day-to-day responsibilities, both organisational and personal, but also trying to reconcile the conflicting demands of different stakeholder groups. Important issues are often poorly analysed, and decisions are taken while under the pressure of time.

Behavioural economics helps us understand why irrational decisions predominate and provides a framework for spotting potential problems and addressing them appropriately. Thinking, from a behavioural perspective, raises our awareness of powerful self-interests and biases with their potential impacts. When we are alert to these behavioural biases, we can incorporate them into our analysis, which will lead, hopefully, to smarter decision-making.

By developing your understanding of biases, both your own and those of others, you raise your awareness and sensitivity to dynamics that can undermine good decision-making. Remember, we are all much better at spotting the biases of other people rather than our own.

## Cognitive Biases

By way of the introduction to biases, let's look at a few common examples that I am confident we are all guilty of most, if not all, of the time. My post-graduate students go through a checklist of 70 biases, (included at the end of this book) and I ask them to tick off those they are aware of having at some time. Without exception, they admit to having exhibited most of them, and that shows they are honest!

The blind spot bias is when we recognise bias in others more easily than in ourselves. Five hundred years ago, Leonardo da Vinci observed, 'It is an acknowledged fact that we perceive errors in the work of others more readily than in our own.'

Today, it is so easy to create and live in our own information bubble. When we subscribe to blogs or news services that support our perspectives, with their inherent biases, those perspectives confirm our opinions and that is known as confirmation bias.

A common bias of leaders, especially those with charisma, is the over-confidence bias. People may become overconfident in their abilities, causing them to take greater risks, and this often happens if an executive has had a series of successes and has garnered media praise. It makes little difference if the success is mainly due to good luck. Interestingly, experts are more prone to the overconfidence bias, and later we will look at illusory superiority and hubris. Overconfidence also links to the halo effect, where a person who is good at one thing is perceived as being good at something else, even though the skills required may be quite different. There is a thin line between con-fidence and overconfidence.

The placebo bias is believing that something will have an effect, and you think you will have the outcome you want. Believing something will hap-pen does not actually impact the likelihood of it happening. An example is claiming that the UK economy would improve after Brexit because of the hope that it would.

When supporters of two different sides in a football match were asked about their team's behaviour, they consistently thought that their own team behaved better.[4] That is known as selective perception.

Anchoring bias is an important factor in negotiations. Whoever sets the initial price anchors the price expectation going forward. For example, we feel elated when we negotiate a big discount off a price even though the ini-tial price might have been inflated to start with.

Returning to Carillion, let's consider some of the biases that might have been affecting the board's decision-making. Here are a few examples but there are many more.

The bandwagon effect, related to groupthink, is when the probability of a belief increases the more people believe it. When a group believes some-thing, particularly when there is a dominant leader, it is challenging for an individual to counter the prevailing view.

Conservatism bias is when things had worked out in the past, so we believe that they will probably be fine this time, too. Perhaps Carillion's pension deficit, powerfully impacted by small changes in inflation and stock market valuations, had balanced itself out in recent years. Richard Adam persuaded the group that things would just work out but without real evidence to support his position.

The ostrich bias most certainly will have been a factor at Carillion because the board didn't want to hear bad news. Zafar Khan, who had been the financial controller under Richard Adam for a couple of years took over the top finance job when Adams retired. When Khan as the new finance director, raised concerns about the accounting policies, he was eventually fired – a powerful warning to other executives of the risk of taking a contrarian position. Senior executives raised concerns privately with Richard Howson but were discouraged from bringing strategic problems into a wider forum.

## Here Are a Few More Common Biases

The hindsight bias, related to the misremembering bias, is when you think a result was inevitable but hold this view after the event has taken place. The House of Commons report on Carillion is full of hindsight bias. However, being wise after an event is easy. Being in the moment and having to make decisions under intense pressure, and guessing how the future will unfold, is intensely challenging. Many times, when there is a satisfactory outcome, we claim success based on ability but, more often, it is just luck. A manifestation of hindsight bias is viewing past events as more predictable than they were.

With misremembering bias, which is a common managerial failing, you blame a subordinate when you made the decision in the first place. And then there is the outcome bias, when we judge a decision on the outcome rather than how the decision was made, again mistaking luck for ability.

There are forces that inhibit change – for example, the status quo bias. This bias encourages inertia because it engenders a strong preference for things to remain the same; and most people resist change, especially when it doesn't lead to a personal advantage. What is known is generally less frightening than the unknown.

Behavioural economists, Daniel Kahneman and Amos Tversky, studied loss aversion and proposed prospect theory. Their research found that losses are twice as painful as gains, and it explains how the fear of a loss impacts our decision-making. There is a rational explanation for this effect. If we have £100 and it falls in value by 50 percent to £50, we need a 100 percent increase in value to get back to where we were.

The disposition effect is the tendency to sell assets that have increased in value, keeping those that have fallen in value. The disposition effect links to prospect theory – we are pleased with the gain but find the loss painful. That is the reason we hold on to losing stock for too long. The fear of loss is very powerful and may explain why we feel safer making no decision rather than accepting our mistakes and taking a loss.

The Dunning-Kruger Effect, also known as illusory superiority or the above average effect, is common in leaders who overestimate their ability. It was named after Professor Justin Kruger, a psychologist at New York University, who observed, 'People who are incompetent are too incompetent to realize how incompetent they are.' Linked to Dunning-Kruger is cognitive bias, when people of lower ability have illusory superiority, and they mistakenly think they have greater cognitive ability than they do. It is a very prevalent bias in leaders in both business and politics and often happens when a person has too much power.

The study by Kruger and Dunning in 1999 identified the illusory superiority bias from the criminal case of McArthur Wheeler. Wheeler robbed banks with his face covered with lemon juice which he believed would make him invisible to the surveillance cameras. That belief was based on his misunderstanding of the chemical properties of lemon juice when used as an invisible ink. Apparently, he was astonished when police came to arrest him. He claimed he had tested the lemon juice before committing the robbery by taking a picture of himself with a Polaroid camera. Dunning said, 'The skills you need to produce a right answer are exactly the skills you need to recognize what a right answer is.'

The master of the universe syndrome is more commonly a male characteristic, and the alpha male often has extreme confidence and self-assurance that have progressed too far. Behavioural characteristics include the belief that they are uniquely gifted to lead and rule. They are never in doubt and treat others with belligerence and aggression. It is easy to spot this type of leader by observing how they run meetings, how they tell their staff what they want to hear, and that they cut dead those who disagree with them.

At the more extreme end of dangerous leadership behaviour are the adrenalin addicts who thrive on risk and danger. An important consequence of this bias is the leader who takes greater risks than they should because they overestimate their ability to hire talent, spot a good investment decision, make correct strategic decisions, etc.

Research by Malmendier and Tate examined CEOs with overconfidence in their abilities and the impacts made on how they managed their companies. It was found that overconfident CEOs are likely to overestimate their abilities to pick successful projects and to run companies. As such, these top managers are likely to invest in too many projects and to overpay for mergers. They found that overconfident CEOs are 55 percent more likely to undertake a merger and, particularly so, if they can finance the deal with internal funds where they can avoid the tough questions from financiers. The overconfidence of employees about company performance is a leading explanation for the provision of stock options for rank-and-file employees.[5]

Framing is a good example of bias affecting decision-making. Identified by Kahneman and Tversky in a ground-breaking study in 1979, framing is viewing a problem by the way choices are described, presented, or framed. With framing, we focus on the advantages or disadvantages of a decision. When we lead the decision in a preferred direction, we are using framing to make one choice look more attractive. Framing is something we all do. For example, a company may claim that 95 percent of their major projects are on time and on budget, but it is unlikely they would boast that 5 percent of their major projects are late and over budget. Or think of the example of yoghurt labelling. We are attracted to the claim of 80 percent fat free and would, most likely, avoid the same product if it was described as 20 percent fat.

The yoghurt example is also misleading because it doesn't tell you how much sugar is in the product. The British Medical Journal pointed out that popular organic yoghurts contain some of the highest sugar levels at 13 g per 100 g, and that is over three teaspoons of sugar. A typical small container of yoghurt is 170 g or equal to about five teaspoons of sugar, hardly healthy and not something we can expect to see on the side of the container of our favourite yogurt.

In the medical world, doctors probably prefer to tell patients that they have a 95 percent survival rate rather than a five percent chance of death from an operation. That is a common example of framing.

The rational economic model predicts that people will have no preference if they are offered, in economic terms, identical choices. For example, 80 percent fat free or 20 percent fat is the same but, as we are now learning to look through a behavioural lens, we can see how our choices are easily distorted or manipulated.

Salience is how noticeable or observable something is. The saliency bias is a tendency to use available traits to make a judgement about a person or situation, focusing on items that are more noticeable and ignoring those that are less so, and creating a bias in favour of things that are striking. For example, the Swiss right wing political party, the neo-Nazi NPD, used the image of black sheep in a herd of white to create a sense of fear over immigration.[6]

The Economist magazine in Britain conducted a survey about perceptions of the levels of various crimes, and the estimates were much higher than actual rates because of news coverage. Consider this comparison: where are you more likely to be murdered – in the United States, Pakistan, or Greenland? Your answer will probably be influenced by recent news stories. In 2016, Greenland had a murder rate of 5.32 per 100,000 compared to 4.96 in the United States in 2018, and 3.88 in Pakistan in 2018. If you fancy a low-risk holiday, Albania's rate was 2.29, Algeria's was 1.36, and Bosnia-Herzegovina had a safe 1.17 per 100,000.[7]

Research by Danish behaviourists, Julian Christensen and Donald Moynihan, looked at motivated reasoning. Motivated reasoning is a phenomenon in social psychology in which emotional biases lead to the justification for a behaviour rather than an accurate reflection of the evidence. The immigration issue used by leave supporters during the Brexit campaign is a good example. The issue appealed to emotions rather than facts.

Politicians seem to agree on the value of evidence-based policymaking. Increasingly, governments test policies by bringing in experts to try to find out what works. In the United Kingdom since the 1960s, governments have used randomised, controlled trials to understand the effectiveness of social programmes and, in the United States, the Evidence-Based Policymaking Act was passed in 2018. What the Danish study discovered was that politicians tended to distort data if it did not support their own biases. In their study, the effectiveness of a social programme was labelled Solution A and Solution B for one group and for another group, the data was labelled as a Government or Private supplied solution. There was consistent interpretation of the data to support the position of the politicians based solely on the labeling. As a test, when politicians were asked to write a paragraph explaining their decision, they doubled down on the misinterpretation. The more experienced the politician, the more they misinterpreted the data. Information tends to be interpreted to support a preconceived position despite the facts.

## Carillion and Behavioural Dynamics

Hanlon's Razer, 'Never attribute to malice that which is adequately explained by stupidity,' is a modern adaption of Goethe's 'Misunderstandings and lethargy produce more wrongs in the world than deceit and malice do, at least the latter two are certainly rarer.' Adapting this adage to organisational strategy, one could say, 'Never attribute to strategy what can be explained by emotion or luck.' Perhaps I am being too cynical.

Another apt quote when thinking about Carillion, is by the American writer and political activist Upton Sinclair (1878–1968). 'It is hard to get a man to understand something when his salary depends on him not understanding it.'

Continuing with our semi-philosophical quotations, Poul Anderson, the American science fiction writer, said, 'I have yet to see any problem, however complicated, when looked at in the right way did not still become more complicated.' And this issue of problem complexity is at the heart of why strategic decisions are so challenging.

In behavioural economics, we look at how someone behaves and try to understand why they are acting that way by examining their motives. We do not look at motives and then attempt to predict behaviour. We focus on behaviour rather than motives as our starting point. For example, Carillion had a policy or behaviour of always increasing dividends, and from that behaviour, we can speculate on what were the motivations behind it. Were the motivations driven by greed, insecurity, or ego? Rising dividends are a factor in supporting a strong share price, and a strong share price increases the value of bonuses and the value of options. A strong share price also makes executives appear and feel successful and competent and is, undoubtedly, more satisfying than the opposite.

## Corporate Culture

Does poor culture create problems, or do problems create the poor culture? Both points have validity. The House of Commons was scathing in its criticism of Carillion's board. They accused the directors of a 'lack of accountability, professionalism and expertise.' But how fair is this? Carillion was a well-established company, having delivered billions of pounds of contracts to demanding clients over a long period of time. Clearly, if they were lacking in expertise or professionalism, the company would not have had such a long run of delivering substantial projects. And, on the point of accountability, the company was audited externally and internally by two leading firms of accountants that delivered detailed annual reports covering all aspects of the business.

Other critical comments from the House of Commons committee include, an 'inward looking culture, culture of non-compliance, culture of making the numbers, and an overly short-term focus.' The Committee criticised the Chairman as an 'unquestioning optimist' and they went on to add that 'senior management pay was not related to long-term performance.' Perhaps the latter is a debatable point. Long-term performance is challenging to measure and reward, and it begs the question of how long is long-term and when is it fair to activate clawback provisions when things go wrong. The House of Commons committee added, 'Corporate culture does not emerge overnight. The chronic lack of accountability and professionalism . . . were failures years in the making.' They also said there was an 'ever-growing reward (for the directors) behind the façade of an ever-growing company.'[8]

## Decision-making and Biases – Five Findings From Psychology

Let's examine five findings from psychology and consider their impact on decision-making and biases. The findings are overconfidence, extreme forecasts, winner's curse, false consensus, and the present bias. Looking at the Carillion case, we see these five factors cropping up time and again.

There is plenty of evidence of overconfidence at Carillion. The executive board members were overconfident about their ability to manage the company and complete successful acquisitions. The management was optimistic about the positive outcome of their projects, thinking they could beat the industry standards. They were overconfident in believing that their cash problems would resolve themselves and that the pension liabilities could be met. In the company's final months, they were confident that the government would bail them out. Carillion's expectations of contract profit were significantly higher than the industry average. If the management had been more introspective, they might have realised that this could only be true if they were cleverer than all their competitors or their numbers were false. The latter explanation turned out to be the case.

Often combined with overconfidence is confirmation bias. People search for confirming rather than disconfirming evidence. Carillion's executives probably saw the ever-rising dividend as evidence of how well they were running the business.

Daniel Kahneman found people were often prepared to make extreme forecasts based on flimsy data. Managerial decision-making is frequently driven by two countervailing, but not necessarily offsetting, biases: bold forecasts (overconfidence) and timid choices. Kahneman suggests this may be linked to loss aversion, as mentioned earlier, when we experience twice the pain of a loss versus the pleasure of a gain, and so we make timid choices. Perhaps the motivator that trumps loss aversion is greed.[9]

Kahneman gives an example of being involved in a major education project to develop a new curriculum. After a year of progress, the team started discussing how long they should expect the rollout of the new curriculum to take. Everyone on the team wrote on a piece of paper their time estimates. The range was from eighteen to thirty months. Kahneman asked one of the distinguished experts in curriculum development how long it had taken for similar projects. The expert said that in the past not all teams had managed to even complete a project, and about 40 percent gave up with the remaining teams taking between seven to ten years. Facing the facts can be demoralising. Nobody had ventured to question the relevance of the forecast.

Winner's curse applies to acquisitions and to contract bids, two central strategies at Carillion. Acquisitions are generally risky activities. Usually, the assets are bought by the group who makes the highest assessment of their value which is often wrong. Carillion clearly overpaid for some acquisitions – for example, by underestimating the risks of the long-term pension liabilities. Winning government Public Finance Initiative (PFI) contracts often generated positive cash flow at the start but, of course, you have to meet long-term liabilities. If a contract is wrongly priced, the early cash flow benefit will eventually be replaced by ongoing contractual losses.

There is an old gambler's adage that if you don't know who the patsy is in the game, it's probably you. On the basis of his story of paying too much for a whistle when he was a child, Benjamin Franklin wrote in 1839, 'A great part of the miseries of mankind were brought upon them by the false estimates they had made of the value of things.'

Was it false consensus when the Carillion board thought that other stakeholders shared their preferences and supported their decisions? Were people widely consulted on decisions? Was there an atmosphere that encouraged debate or one that stifled dissenting opinions? Several former Carillion executives have reported that alternative debate was strongly discouraged. Were people afraid to challenge decisions or sidelined? Sidelining is a common characteristic with leaders who are bullies and insecure. A colleague who was a senior executive at Blackrock recounted a pension fund meeting where the director shouted and ridiculed everyone because their assessment of the situation was negative, and that didn't fit with the macho bravado culture of the group.

The last of our five findings is the present bias. Everyone wants to win now, believing that the latest deal will immediately turn things around and make the problems disappear.

These five decision-making factors are common in organisations. The boards of listed companies are under enormous pressure to perform and meet or beat quarterly, half-yearly, and annual expectations. It's not surprising that, as well as manipulating grey-area accounting, executives fall prey to psychological delusion.

## Carillion – Hubris and More

I would like to expand our review of behavioural factors affecting Carillion's leaders and dig into that common and dangerous personality trait, hubris.

Charles Handy describes hubris as, 'A Greek word that translates to overweening pride, is something that comes before a fall, it is based on self-interest, short-termism and myopia.' Hubris is extreme or excessive pride in one's own accomplishments, a rather fitting description of Carillion's board executives.

The House of Commons report highlighted that the board, 'Took a lot of pride in their dividend paying track record,' adding that there was 'wilful blindness by long-serving staff.' The CEO demonstrated misguided self-assurance, at least in public, and acted as a cheerleader for the company. The House report said the board, 'showed a high level of self-confidence in their own ability.' You will recall that misplaced high levels of self-confidence are called the Dunning-Kruger effect. As things started to unravel for Carillion, there was plenty of blame transference which, in behavioural terms, is called the fundamental attribution error.

The *Financial Times* writer, Tim Hartford, in *Messy: How to Be Creative and Resilient in a Tidy-Minded World*, suggested developing a hubris checklist. He recommended looking at how are dissenting voices treated, what is their attitude to compliance, how easily does the boss get irritated and, finally, suggests that you shouldn't invest in a company named after someone. Jane Hendy, the Dean of Brunel University Business School, wrote, 'We think of hubris as the behaviour of an individual, but there can be a contamination effect where hubris spreads through an organisation and where it can get much bigger and become out of control.'

Blame transference is common. We all do it. For example, it is when you credit hard work for your success and blame external forces outside your control for failures.

The House of Commons Report noted, 'Rather than a failure of management, the collapse of Carillion was, to them, the fault of their advisers, the Bank of England, the foreign exchange markets, Brexit, the snap 2017 General Election, Carillion's investors, Carillion's suppliers, the entire UK construction industry, Middle Eastern business culture, the construction market of Canada, and professional designers of concrete beams.' 'In their evidence to us, Carillion's directors gave no indication that they accepted any blame for their decisions that ultimately led to the collapse of the company. They sought to point the finger at anyone or anything else they could find, to blame everyone but themselves for the destruction they caused. Their expressions of regret offer no comfort for employees, former employees and suppliers who have suffered because of their failure of leadership.'

In 1979, Nobel Prize winners Kahneman and Tversky presented their prospect theory. Prospect theory posits that people are more risk-averse when doing well, and more risk seeking when making losses. People become less risk-averse than normal – that is, they are actively risk-seeking when things are going badly, and this behaviour becomes exaggerated when gambling with other people's money. If they think there is a chance of getting back to a winning position, a devil-may-care attitude can lead to dangerous risk taking and a what-the-heck, in-for-a-penny-in-for-a pound mindset. As an example, traders take bigger risks near the end of the year when they are behind their benchmark.[10]

Applying prospect theory, Carillion's management were probably taking bigger gambles on potentially loss-making projects, hoping that they could make up for the losses generated by unprofitable and failing projects. And was the unwillingness to rectify the pension fund deficit based on the unfounded hope that things would just miraculously work out?

What were the signs of this increased risk-taking at Carillion? They made bullish public statements when the underlying performance was deteriorating and were motivated by incentives to present a hugely optimistic picture. Major problems were covered up, and they turned a blind eye to poor practices. Eventually, as the situation became more desperate, there was lying and holding back on bad news and, in the end, employees, suppliers, customers, pensioners, and investors were defrauded.

Kahneman makes another important psychological observation. He states, 'Judgments of relatively inaccessible factors are expected to be substantially slower and more susceptible to interference by concurrent mental activity, in comparison to judgments of accessible attributes.'

When the Carillion directors were under mounting pressure to address increasing write-offs and nonperforming contracts, and banks and pension advisors were pressing for changes, and debtors were delaying payment, was their reasoning impaired? Was it more difficult, as Kahneman suggests, to focus on the big picture and tackle fundamental problems because the immediate challenges dominated the attention of the directors?

## A Deeper Consideration of Bounded Rationality

I would like to expand our review of psychological factors and how they link to individual rationality in decision-making.

Herbert Simon, the Nobel Prize-winning organisational thinker, described the area of rationality when he wrote,

> When the limits to rationality are viewed from the individual's standpoint, they fall into three categories; 1. The limits by our unconscious skills, habits, and reflexes; 2. The limitations imposed by our values and conceptions of purpose, these 'conceptions of purpose' may diverge from the organisation goals; 3. We are limited by the extent of our knowledge and information. Rationality therefore does not determine behaviour; behaviour is determined by the irrational and nonrational elements that bound the area of rationality.[11]

So, here we have two ideas about rationality. Simon talking about zones or areas of rationality, and Richard Thaler describing Bounded Rationality, a term incidentally coined by Simon in 1957, as our limited ability to deal with complex problems. We compensate for these human limitations by using mental shortcuts or heuristics. The problems of Bounded Rationality are exacerbated by external pressures. Just think how you react in a restaurant when making a choice, and the waiter is standing over you clearly in a rush. Or, a more serious example, a CEO dealing with significant current problems who will experience greater difficulty dealing with complex strategic issues.

In the Ernst & Young consultant's report produced at the end of 2017, they present a model of Carillion's business. Carillion was complex. They undertook large, logistically complicated, multi-year contracts with diverse customers including governments, quasi-government agencies, and the private sector across multiple geographies. For outstanding executives with a highly functional culture, this type of business is challenging to manage. Carillion,

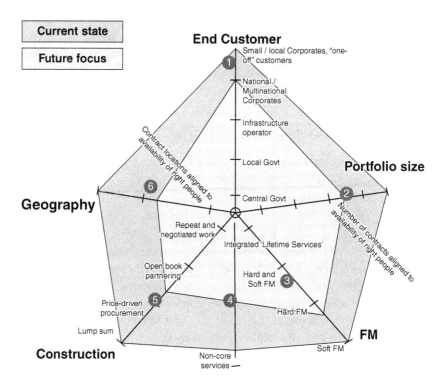

Figure 4.1  Carillion market position – EY Internal Strategy Report Jan 2018.[12]

however, had a board with two executives who, by all accounts, were out of their depth and, in addition, were constrained by a closed culture and a bottleneck of information flowing to the top.

In a typical board meeting, lasting perhaps for a few hours, is it reasonable to think that non-executive directors (NEDs) can make meaningful contributions to a debate about important issues facing such a complex business model?

Veteran Wall Street investor, Peter Lynch, advised, 'Go for a business that any idiot can run – because sooner or later any idiot probably is going to be running it.'[13] Was Carillion so complicated that it was not a question of an idiot running the business but that such a challenging business needed to be managed by a team of geniuses?

John Flannery, a former CEO of General Electric in America who managed 283,000 employees and $300 billion in assets spread across a vast industrial and financial business said, 'Management thinking will only take you so far when the structure you have built is unmanageable.'[14]

At some point, Carillion became unmanageable.

## Heuristics

Heuristics are rules of thumb that help us make decisions. They are a tool to handle Bounded Rationality. However, heuristics cause people to make predictable errors. The first consequence of the principle of Bounded Rationality is that the intended rationality requires you to construct a simplified model of the real situation in order to deal with it. We say that these simplified mental models are heuristics.

Two common mental short-cuts are satisficing – searching for information about alternatives until an option is found that is good enough – and the elimination by aspects – deciding on some key features that matter and ignoring options that do not meet a baseline threshold.[15]

Kahneman and Tversky described the availability heuristic that is based on how easy it is to bring something to mind. Here is an example. Do more words occur in the English language starting with the letter K, or are there more words where the third letter is a K? The correct answer is that there are more English words with K as a third letter, and it is three times more common. We mentally switch the question about frequency to how easily an answer comes to mind. Words starting with K are much easier to recall quickly, and we assume that something is probably more common because you can bring it to mind easily.

Another example is that, when people were asked how many murders took place in Essex in a year, respondents guessed between ten and twenty. The actual answer for that year was two, but because news of a murder is dramatic and sensational, we assume that there are many.

The availability heuristic is often used when we are asked about the frequency of events. It explains why people are more frightened of flying than of driving although the risk is much higher in a car. Yet another example is drug advertisements that mention symptoms such as fatigue or headaches. We can all remember having a headache or feeling tired.

Kahneman in 2003 pointed out the opposite of the availability heuristic, 'Judgments of relatively inaccessible properties are expected to be substantially slower and more susceptible to interference by concurrent mental activity, in comparison to judgments of accessible attributes.'[16]

In his bestselling book, *Thinking Fast and Slow*, Kahneman wrote about System 1 and System 2 thinking processes. 'When making decisions, humans rely to a great extent on automatic, effortless, affective (moods/feelings), subconscious and the associative side of human judgment and decision-making.' He contrasts quick System 1 processes with the controlled, effortful, deductive, conscious, and rule-based System 2 processes.[17] System 1 thinking, the fast decision process, is easily distorted by common biases such as the availability bias. Information that quickly comes to mind crowds out better answers, and we often attempt to answer a difficult question by substituting an easier one. Prejudgement leads to distorting new information in favour of an initial judgement, and conclusion bias can lead to bypassing new evidence.

> At the core of behavioural economics is the insight that humans do not behave in line with the assumptions of rationality postulated by standard economic theory. In contrast, humans display bounded rationality[18] enabling the situational context of an individual or group to influence their behaviour.[19]

Kahneman and Tversky found that, when making judgements about the probability of an event under uncertainty, we are likely to judge wrongly because the fact that something is representative of an event does not make it the same as the current problem. We are using a mental shortcut because something looks like something we have experienced, and we apply that experience to the new decision but fail to carefully observe and consider the differences.

Here are a couple of examples. I have interviewed a hundred people – seventy lawyers and thirty librarians. I mix up my notes of the interviewees and pull one out. Sheila is fifty-three years old, having worked at the same place for fifteen years. She wears thick glasses, spends much of her time reading, and likes a quiet work environment. Is she likely to be a librarian or a lawyer? We are poor at calculating the odds of an event, so we use a representative image of a stereotypical librarian. We are not doing the math but there is a 70 percent chance that a person selected at random in our sample will be a lawyer. We are just mentally asking how this description matches a prototypical image and probably arriving at a false conclusion.

Another example is that Bob tours museums and galleries when he goes on holiday. Is Bob: A – a person who plays trumpet and is in a local orchestra; or B – a farmer. One probability is more likely, and most people guess A. This is an opportunity to mention Bayes, who my university is now named after. Bayes Theorem explains why Bob in the above example is more likely to be a farmer, and that in the calculation of conditional probabilities, the factors are multiplied. Also, when we are interviewed for a job, we are often assessed by our representativeness to an employee the interviewer liked or didn't like, rather than who we are.

It should be remembered that how confidently you express a position is not the same as the probability of it being correct. We will explore later the dangers of leaders who are overconfident and charismatic.

## Behavioural Factors – A Few Additional Points

Before moving on to explore risks, let me round up this section on behavioural factors by reviewing a few thoughts on money, motivation, and self-control.

When an amount of money has been spent and the money cannot be retrieved, money is said to be sunk. Economic theory would suggest that, in general, these costs should be ignored; however, sunk costs may also have ego costs which are not so easily written off. Barry Staw, who researched organisational decision-making, found that leaders tended to stick with, and increase investment in, their preferred projects even when the evidence was clear that it was time to move on. Staw called this pattern 'escalating commitment,' a similar idea to Drucker's 'investment in management ego.' Staw suggests three de-escalation procedures that were found to be most effective: first, making negative outcomes less threatening; second, setting minimum target levels that, if not achieved, would lead to a change of policy; and third, evaluating decision-makers on their processes rather than on the outcome.[20]

Carillion had £1.6 billion in goodwill on their balance sheet. This goodwill represented the premium they paid over the net asset value of their acquisitions. To write-off or write-down that figure would have been a public admission of their mistakes. It takes a lot of courage for a board to admit serious errors of judgement and to deal with the likely market punishment, and that was something the directors of Carillion were not prepared to do.

We behave differently and irrationally when gambling with money we have won, known as house money, and also with other people's money. These forms of money burn a hole in our pockets and encourage an easy come, easy go mentality. Thaler discusses this in the 'Economic Theory of Self-Control,' highlighting the difference between thinking as managers versus owners. Interestingly, when people think about their own money, they become more concerned with being treated fairly.[21] Although we think that money is the most powerful of motivations for ambitious executives, a former insider at Carillion said, 'My perception, from close observation, is that self-preservation was a greater motivator than bonuses.'

The expectation bias is linked to the placebo effect mentioned earlier. By hoping something will happen, you falsely believe that it is more likely to happen. Did Carillion think that the pension liability would go away, which increased their confidence that it would? We actively ignore dangerous or negative information, but it doesn't change the probabilities.

Creeping normality is when a significant problem doesn't cause alarm because the change happens slowly.

Thaler observed that 'most people realize they have self-control issues but underestimate their severity,' and that we are naive about the level of 'mental sophistication' we use to avoid rational self-control. Self-control is essentially about conflict.

Investors like doers and go-getter entrepreneurs, and stories about growth and dynamism are exciting. Investors tend to look less favourably on the calmer, forward-looking, planner-type leader – Kahneman's System 2 thinker. The pressure on Carillion's leaders to be winners was no doubt relentless, and they knew they had to play to the gallery.

## Notes

1 Dan Ariely and Simon Jones, *The (Honest) Truth About Dishonesty: How We Lie to Everyone-Especially Ourselves* (New York: Harper Collings, 2012); P. Donal et al., 2012.
2 Herbert Simon, *Administrative Behaviour*, 4th ed. (New York: Free Press, 1997), 420.
3 M. G. Haselton and D. Nettle, "The Paranoid Optimist," *Personality and Social Psychology Review* 10, no. 1 (2006): 47–66.
4 H. Cantril, *The 'Why' of Man's Experience* (New York: Macmillan, 1950).
5 Ulrike Malmendier and Geoffrey Tate, *Who Makes Acquisitions? CEO Overconfidence and the Market's Reaction*, Working Paper 10813 (Cambridge, MA: National Bureau of Economic Research, September 2004).
6 Daniel Kahneman et al., 1982; Bordalo et al., 2012; Allcott and Wozny, 2013.
7 www.indexmundi.com/facts/indicators/VC.IHR.PSRC.P5/rankings.
8 HoC 769, 53.
9 Daniel Kahneman and Dan Lovallo, "Timid Choices and Bold Forecasts: A Cognitive Perspective on Risk Taking," *Management Science* 39, no. 1 (1993): 17–31.
10 Richard Thaler, *Misbehaving* (New York: W. W. Norton, 2016).
11 Simon, *Administrative Behaviour*, 323.
12 www.parliament.uk/globalassets/documents/commons-committees/work-and-pensions/Carillion-Group-Business-Plan-January-2018.pdf.
13 Quoted in interview with USA today 1989 and attributed to Warren Buffett.
14 *FT*, June 30, 2018.
15 A. Tversky, "Elimination by Aspects: A Theory of Choice," *Psychological Review* 79, no. 4 (1972): 281–99.
16 Daniel Kahneman, "A Perspective on Judgment and Choice: Mapping Bounded Rationality," *American Psychologist* 58, no. 9 (2003): 697–720.
17 Daniel Kahneman, *Thinking, Fast and Slow* (New York: Farrar, Straus and Giroux, 2011).
18 Kahneman, "A Perspective on Judgment and Choice"; Simon, *Administrative Behaviour*.
19 Ariely and Jones; Donal et al.
20 I. Simonson and B. M. Staw, "De-Escalation Strategies: A Comparison of Techniques for Reducing Commitment To Losing Courses of Action," *Journal of Applied Psychology* 77, no. 4 (1992): 419–26.
21 Thaler, *Misbehaving*, 267.

# 5

## RISK

Risk is everywhere, and risk can be paradoxical. The more we avoid risk, the less we do – which may be riskier – so, we have the risk of action and the risk of inaction. When not properly understood, risk can lead to disaster, and even when properly understood, you take the risk you might have a disaster anyway.

Corporate strategy is inextricably linked to risk because strategy leads to choices, choices force decisions, and decisions involve risk. The level of risk we can tolerate is situation dependent. The failure of a new aircraft designed by Boeing is not the same as the corporate risk for Ford when a new model fails. The failure of a major investment for a cash-rich firm is completely different if the same size project fails for a firm that is cash-strapped. Throwing $44 billion on the table for a business you don't fully understand may be less of a risk if you are the richest businessman in the world. So, our challenge is not about avoiding risk but to understand, quantify, and manage it.

I am going to explore risk as it relates to corporate strategy and decision-making, not portfolio or mathematical finance because those are technical

DOI: 10.4324/9781003457398-6

subjects outside the scope of this book. Strategic risks are hard to model and quantify because they involve the unknown and the unknowable future, and they involve anticipating the behaviour of uncontrollable actors including customers, governments, competitors, economies, and investors. This unknowability is what makes corporate strategy so challenging.

Because we deal with unknowns and an unknowable future, the best we can do is make broad guesses about what to do and what the outcomes might be. The problem of fog obscuring our future is compounded because our operating environment is dynamic, not static, and everyone is reacting to new information in different and often unpredictable ways. As we have discussed earlier, external actors are unlikely to be making rational decisions and are subject to all the whims, caprices, inconsistencies, biases, and blundering as the rest of us.

However reasonable our plans may be, people do not like change or uncertainty and will resist changes that they perceive to be against their self-interest. Change involves risk and uncertainty. It makes most people psychologically uncomfortable and is rarely to everyone's advantage. It leads to a different constellation of winners and losers, and the losers will actively or passively resist and try to delay, sabotage, or derail anything that is to their disadvantage.

Nicolo Machiavelli (1469–1527) wrote,

> There is nothing more difficult to take in hand, more perilous to conduct, or more uncertain in its success, than to take the lead in the introduction of a new order of things. Because the innovator has for enemies all those who have done well under the old conditions, and lukewarm defenders in those who may do well under the new.

How accurately can we measure strategic risk? What are the probabilities of various outcomes – 1 percent, 10 percent, 20 percent, or more? Unfortunately, investors, accountants, statisticians, and economists like accuracy, so we often see precise predictions that are really little more than guesses. For example, in March 2020 the UK Office of Budget Responsibility (OBR) forecast CPI inflation for 2023 at about 2 percent. In March 2021, they forecast it at 2.5 percent; and in March 2022, the forecast was 8 percent. Another OBR forecast estimated GDP growth of 1.7 percent in 2026 – yet we have no idea about the price of energy supplies, wage inflation, or which political party will be in power.[1] A more honest forecast would be a range of numbers without decimal places. The danger is that by giving a precise number, we infer a level of accuracy to our predictions that are simply based on too many variables. This inference of accuracy is frequently unreliable and misleading.

Fire Chief Sabrina Cohen-Hatton wrote about what she learned about decision-making under pressure in her book, In the Heat of the Moment, and based her Ph.D. on the subject. She found that 80 percent of Fire Service accidents were because of human error, avoidable mistakes, poor decisions, and misunderstood risks. That 80 percent might apply to strategic decisions because, frequently, these decisions are taken under pressure. That was certainly the case at Carillion in the years before the collapse.

Luck, rather than skill, probably accounts for more satisfactory outcomes than anything else. When things turn out well, we claim skill was responsible and, when things go wrong, that it was just bad luck. Remember the saying, 'When history is written, the laurel leaves are awarded.'

Survivor bias is where we focus on examples of successful outcomes but exclude those that didn't survive. We read about heroes who took a big risk and won, but we don't hear much about the rest – the majority. Most very successful people have taken great risks. Those are the stories we remember, that we hear about in the media, and that are highlighted in business school case studies. Survivorship bias leads to false conclusions about performance and encourages optimistic thinking. For example, an investment company might launch ten funds. After three years, perhaps a third are doing badly so they are closed. The remaining funds appear to be performing better than average because the surviving two-thirds are now 100 percent of the funds.

During the Second World War, statistician Abraham Wald at Columbia University showed that research by the Center for Naval Analysis had come to an incorrect conclusion. They had mapped out where bombers were damaged on their fuselage with an intention of adding more protective armour to the aircraft. Wald pointed out that they needed to look at the lost aircraft, not those that returned.

Frank Knight, an American economist whose ideas about risk are known as Knightian uncertainty, was one of the founders of the Chicago School of Economics. In 1921, Knight wrote his classic work on economic theory, Risk, Uncertainty and Profit. He looked at new opportunities where we have imperfect knowledge of future events. He said that risk applies when we do not know the outcome but can accurately measure the odds. However, he used the word, uncertainty, when we cannot know all the information to set accurate odds. There is a fundamental difference in taking a risk when the odds are known, versus uncertainty that has unknown odds. Knight pointed out that true risk is not susceptible to measurement. Some economists argue that this distinction is misleading as all events are so complex that forecasting is always a matter of true uncertainty. We may well have a good handle on the risks if a certain outcome happens, but we don't know how to calculate the odds of that outcome taking place.

Daniel Ellsberg, a behavioural psychologist, pointed out in his work on ambiguity aversion in 1962 that people prefer a bet with a probability of success versus one without even if the alternative might be better. Ellsberg points out that we are uncomfortable with ambiguity and that we can relieve the psychological discomfort that comes from uncertainty. He wrote that any decision, even the obviously wrong one, is preferred to no decision because it relieves the anxiety caused by the necessity to decide. Perhaps this goes some way to explain the outcome of Brexit. People just wanted to get it over with, even if the decision was bad, and some politicians understood that and encouraged the 'Get it Done' slogan.

There is a danger that our fear of risk becomes paralyzing. The behavioural implications are that we put off decisions, go for default, let someone else take the decision, or, as I said above, just make a decision for the sake of ending the anxiety.

## Risk and Bernoulli

Theories of decision-making go back to Daniel Bernoulli (1700–1782). Bernoulli, a Swiss mathematician and physicist, pioneered work on statistics and probability. He is credited with inventing the idea of risk aversion.

Bernoulli observed that people have a diminishing marginal utility of wealth, meaning that the more you have, the less you are bothered about getting more unless the increase is significant to you. This doesn't mean people can't be cheap or obsessively greedy. This idea of diminishing marginal utility raises the question of utility or value for whom? Utility for one group may be a disadvantage for another – for example, cost-cutting to boost profits versus employees losing jobs in the name of efficiency.

Bernoulli wrote, 'An investor's acceptance of risk should incorporate not only the possible losses that can occur, but also the utility or intrinsic value of the investment itself.' He added, 'The desirability of the preference that an organisation has for a given outcome is dependent on the reference point from which the possible gain or loss will occur, rather than on the final value of the assets that will result.'

Applying Bernoulli's ideas to the situation facing the directors of Carillion, they may have been focusing on gains or losses that impacted themselves or on their personal time-frames rather than the expectations of stakeholders. Significant long-term decisions that can enhance short-term performance but carry long term risk, when taken close to a senior executive's retirement require particularly careful consideration.

Kahneman's prospect theory shifts the focus from levels of wealth to changes in wealth. Change is the way humans experience life. If we are doing well, our attitude towards taking big risks is not the same as if things are going badly. If things are going wrong, we often mistakenly believe a grand gesture is called for with meaningless idioms such as what the heck, in for a penny in for a pound, fortune favours the brave, or nothing ventured nothing gained – all of which may be used to justify a risky strategy.

Remember, at Carillion the board knew things were not going well. There was pressure to keep the good news flowing, and they must have sensed the danger until the problems became too big to hide.

In *Antifragile* (2014), Nassim Taleb talks about skin in the game. It is a useful way of thinking about what risks people are taking. For example, when fund managers who are selling investment products talk about risk, they mean your risk and not theirs. It explains why people take bigger risks when using other people's money, particularly when there is asymmetry between the downside and the upside. You could argue that is what led to the 2008 financial crash when too many people working in the finance industry enjoyed massive rewards whilst taking very little personal risk.

In the risk-reward equation, we need to understand who is taking the risk and who gets the utility or reward because they are often not the same. In Carillion's case, who was taking the risk and who was getting the utility?

Kahneman pointed out in *Thinking Fast and Slow* (2012) that 'it is easier to see other people's mistakes than our own.' The takeaway from that is that it is important to work hard to recognise situations where mistakes are more likely, especially where stakes are high and the risk is unfairly distributed.

In summary, risk aversion or risk taking depends on the amount involved, how much better off or worse off you may become, and the relative impact on your present positions. It is useful to keep in mind the trap of cognitive ease, that we are more open to an idea that is easy to understand – for example, being sold on something by a slick presentation. Remember the opposite case of 'let's not dismiss this business plan because the font is hard to read.' Risks don't diminish because an idea is superficially appealing or packaged with a snappy message.

## Risking Other People's Money

Let's dig deeper into how peoples' risk-taking behaviour may be impacted by financial incentives. It is an important topic because understanding what motivations are influencing decision-makers will help us identify where conflicts of interest may benefit one group of stakeholders whilst harming others.

Andrew Haldane, the former Chief Economist of the Bank of England, wrote,

> To motivate decision-makers, the authority to take decisions on behalf of others is often coupled with powerful incentives. A basic problem with this practice is that it is typically hard to construct compensation schemes that perfectly align the incentives of decision-makers with the interests of other stakeholders. Haldane argues that the banking sector's problems are rooted in the fact that the private risks of financial decision-makers are not aligned with social risks, and the latter, are of a much greater magnitude.[2]

A paper by Ola Andersson et al (2019) found decision-makers often face powerful incentives to increase risk-taking on behalf of others either through bonus contracts or through competitive relative performance contracts. The authors found that people respond to such incentives without much concern for stakeholders. Responses were somewhat mitigated by personality traits. The findings suggest that a lack of concern for the risk exposure of others hardly requires financial psychopaths to flourish but is diminished by social concerns. The paper's two main findings were: first, ordinary people respond to powerful incentives to take risks without much apparent concern for what this entails for investors, called receivers by the researchers.

Bonus schemes trigger increased risk-taking on behalf of others only when the returns of receivers are negatively correlated. Hence, a bonus scheme with well-aligned risk profiles between decision-makers and receivers does not distort risk-taking. Competition, on the other hand, triggers increased risk-taking irrespective of the structure of receiver returns. For the receiver, competition between the decision-makers thereby always leads to higher risk exposure.

> Measures of personality and pro-social orientation explain risk-taking on behalf of others rather well. Individuals who have low scores in these dimensions expose receivers to significantly more risk. Ordinary people tend to do it when the incentives of decision-makers and receivers are not aligned. The general lesson is that policy makers should become more circumspect in designing incentives and institutions, because they impact the risks that are taken on behalf of others.

The research found strong support that competition and bonus when paired with hedged payoff schemes create particularly strong incentives for risk-taking.

> Neither age nor educational level shows any significant predictive power for risking other people's money. Females seem to take more risks on behalf of others. Self-employed people tend to make fewer safe choices. An important finding is that taking increased risk with other people's money applies to perfectly regular people. The second important finding is that pro-social behaviour, altruism, moderates our propensity to risk other people's money.[3]

Kleinlercher et al. (2014) found that incentives have a huge impact on investment behaviour. Their study suggests that high-powered incentives are strong drivers for making risky choices with other people's money, and they crowd out the moral imperative of responsible decision-making.

The evidence from these studies is clear that financial incentive schemes can easily distort performance to the determent of investors or shareholders, and great care is needed to align rewards for executives that allow them to enrich themselves at the expense of those they are paid to serve.,[45]

## Asymmetric Risk

Asymmetric risk is an interesting perspective for contextualising the decisions that are often made by senior executives and, particularly, by fund managers. Asymmetric risk means that one party − for example, a fund manager − has low risk if things go wrong and a high upside if it all works out. The other party − say, an investor − has either high or low returns, depending on how things go, but always higher risk when things go wrong. The key point is that the risk and reward are unevenly distributed between the two parties, and we need to be on the lookout for asymmetry when we observe one side advocating a certain strategy.

In August 2021, Sports Direct made headlines. The incoming boss, the future son-in-law of the high-profile and controversial founder, Mike Ashley, was offered a staggering pay deal − £100 million if he could double the share price in three years. Let's consider some factors that might impact the share price doubling: perhaps the UK stock market will double anyway in that time; could profits be ramped up in the short term at the expense of future business performance; what if the new CEO is a genius but factors beyond his control result in the share price not doubling. Will there be pressure to push grey area accounting if the numbers are close to tripping the big payout? After all, £100 million is a pretty big incentive for any sort of nefarious behaviour. This sort of arrangement is clearly asymmetrical. If the share price doubles, the son-in-law wins big time and so do the shareholders, assuming they sell their shares at the peak. But if the shares double by the target date and then quickly drop in value, presumably the new CEO keeps his massive payout anyway.

A classic investment definition of asymmetric risk is the risk an investor faces when the gain realised from the move of an underlying asset in one direction is significantly different from the loss incurred from its move in the opposite direction.

Consider the asymmetric risk for the directors of Carillion. If the share price and dividends stayed high, their salary, and bonuses would continue to rise. An executive who is about to retire is in a subtly different position because their time frame is short. The former CFO, Richard Adam, had a clear incentive to maintain a high share price in the short term because, when he retired in 2016, he could sell his share options when he left the company. What happens to Carillion and the share price after Adam sells his shares has no impact on his wealth.

There is a strong incentive for an executive who is close to retirement to do everything possible to keep the share price as high as possible in the short term. Financially, the collapse of a company, apart from some ego embarrassment, has no impact on the wealth of a retired, cashed-out director. Later, we will consider psychological factors that impact how we justify our behaviour to ourselves and others and that can blind us to the real reasons for our actions.

## Risk and a Few More Thoughts

We have looked at our attitude towards risk and how biases and incentives can distort our behaviour, producing unintended consequences.

There is an adage that greed and fear drive stock markets, but I think greed is the more powerful of the two. Decision-makers focus on a perceived return which is easier to estimate than a risk-adjusted return and which is what really matters. In business, the estimated return and the risk-adjusted return are rarely the same.

You will recall that the overconfidence bias leads to taking greater risks. The opposite, a lack of confidence, of course impacts our attitude to risk, too. One way to defend against these biases is to have a strong and empowered team.

Hans Rosling, in his book, *Factfulness*, warned, 'Beware of comparisons of averages, beware comparisons of extremes and beware grouping of data into significantly different groups.' Here's an example from the United States. On average, almost 4.5 million people are injured or killed on the roads. In fact, about 1 percent of the 4.5 million or 46,000 are killed. The rest are injured, a tragically high number but, by adding the injured to the killed numbers, the news story paints a highly distorted picture.

The straight-line instinct is when we assume that graphs continue in a straight line. However, straight lines are less common than we think. There are other more commonly-shaped curves that fit data. There are the S curves where things start slowly and then increase, then plateau, and then decline, and that is a common shape of the graph for the performance of many companies. There is the normal distribution curve or frequency distribution that is common in nature. There is the doubling or geometric curve, a hockey stick shape often seen in start-up business plans. In fact, almost every start-up uses a hockey stick projection to justify their high valuation. From my experience, the hockey stick curve for early-stage businesses is better flipped horizontally with a steady rise as funds are spent and then a dramatic drop when the hoped-for returns fail to materialise. The warning is to be cautious in putting the line you expect onto a projection.

A key element when thinking about risk is how do we quantify it? We must deal with the known, unknown, and unknowable. Taleb's black swan events that, incidentally, can be both good and bad, are positive or negative events that are deemed improbable yet cause massive consequences. Jim Robison, a former CEO of several Bain & Company investments, believes that black swan events are much more common than we think but that our capacity to address them is underestimated, too. That presumes that a black swan event is not so catastrophic that an organisation cannot survive.

In the context of Carillion, there wasn't a black swan event. There was a long series of poor strategic decisions that created increasing risk that was not addressed and, finally, created so much pressure that the business collapsed.

One thing is clear. We do not spend enough time thinking about risk, perhaps because thinking is hard work, takes time, and delays action. Certainly, in the strategic decision context, risk can be very difficult or impossible to measure, but it is a useful exercise to put a number on the percentage probability of being right or wrong. Any guess is better than no guess. An essential question to ask when thinking about risk is what are the consequences of being right or wrong.

There is an allure of the big bet. We all know the image of James Bond at the roulette wheel. Powerful, cool, macho – and I suspect there is something of that persona involved when executives take big and often reckless gambles. As we discussed earlier, if the big bet pays off, the winner claims it is all down to skill – but when it fails, the culprit is bad luck.

Behaviourists highlight some biases related to risk taking. Misremembering is common. If a risk pays off, a leader will take the credit but, if it fails, the blame will be apportioned elsewhere. Thaler pointed out that the laurels usually go to the most famous or important member of the team. Another example is hindsight bias, the we-knew-it-all-along bias.

A frequent psychological failing is thinking that what you don't see is not there, and what you don't understand does not exist. Kahneman points out, 'We're not aware of changing our minds even when we do change our minds. And most people, after they change their minds, reconstruct their past opinion – they believe they always thought that.'

Taleb suggests that looking at fragility is a good way of thinking about risk. Antifragile structures, according to Taleb, are those categories of things that not only gain from chaos but also need it in order to survive and flourish. He suggests building antifragility into an organisation's structure to make it more resilient and robust – not only able to resist shocks but able to gain from them. Why is it difficult for organisations to build antifragile structures? Building robustness in an organisation is expensive in the short term and has a short-term profit impact. The benefits take time to accrue and are often hard to measure until it is too late, as in Carillion's case perhaps. Most shareholders have little appetite for short-term loss over potential longer-term gain, so building antifragility needs managers who have a long-term vision for their organisation's success and the ability to sell their ideas to investors. If Carillion had been building an antifragile structure, what might they have done differently?

How should we address and manage risk? With strategic risk, we must ask the big question of how much is at stake if it all goes wrong. Because, often, everything does.

Insurance is a useful tool to mitigate risk, however, it is a wide topic so I mention it briefly rather than tackle the subject in any depth. I'm using the word, insurance, to mean more than just buying a policy. Let me give you an example. Lucius Servianus (45–136 AD) lived until he was ninety-one, and that was a very respectable age for anyone in ancient Rome. He was an ambitious Roman politician and attempted the risky strategy to limit Hadrian's efforts to be the chosen heir of Emperor Trajan. Servianus was a pragmatic fellow and became reconciled with Hadrian when Hadrian was appointed Emperor. Hadrian, as a brilliant politician, treated Servianus with distinguished honour and, for a time, considered Servianus might be his heir. Things changed, and Hadrian had another person in mind as his inheritor. As a piece of insurance, Hadrian retained a spy in Servianus's household in order to keep an eye on the contender just in case Servianus's loyalty changed.[6]

I want to mention compliance as a side note to our discussion about risk. Compliance is a bane for many large organisations from health care to finance. Risk management has become confused with compliance, and we have muddled up real risk versus compliance or noncompliance risk. All quoted companies must provide investors with a detailed report in their annual accounts for the risks they face and what they are doing to mitigate them.

Carillion's accounts contain extensive disclosure of the risks the business faced. Perhaps the disclosures in the accounts made executives feel they were addressing risk, but a disclosure does not address risk. It just identifies it. It's worth considering whether the directors of Carillion were confusing their compliance by disclosing risks without taking real action to mitigate them.

In the 2016 accounts, Carillion lists the top three riskiest items: work winning, contract management, and pension liabilities. On page 142 of the report, these three factors are closely clustered on the Group's Principal Risk chart. Contract management, a term that includes not just managing contracts but winning them at an economic price, and the pension shortfall were significant factors in the company's demise and were clearly shown as high risk. A question that we raised before is how come, with all this risk disclosure, how did the analysts and professional investors so misprice this stock? Clearly, identifying risk is not the same as addressing it.

As Kay and King point out,

> Risk factors may well be reviewed and clearly noted but rarely are they incorporated into strategic plans and they are even less likely to be carefully mitigated. It is almost as if noting the risk is somehow going to magically make it less dangerous.

Was this the case at Carillion? The risks were clearly stated for anyone interested enough to read the accounts, but what did the executive team really do to address the risks over and above just identifying them?

## Notes

1  OBR Economic and Fiscal Outlook, March 2022.
2  A. Haldane and R. May, "Systemic Risk in Banking Ecosystems," *Nature* 469 (2011): 351–55.
3  Ola Andersson, Håkan J. Holm, Jean-Robert Tyran, and Erik Wengström, "Risking Other People's Money: Experimental Evidence on Bonus Schemes, Competition and Altruism," *The Scandinavian Journal of Economics* 122 (March 18, 2019).

4 Sujoy Chakravarty, Glenn W. Harrison, Ernan E. Haruvy, and E. Elisabet Rutström, "Are You Risk Averse Over Other People's Money?" *Southern Economic Journal* 77 (2011): 901–13; S. Frederick, "Cognitive Reflection and Decision-making," *Journal of Economic Perspectives* 19 (2005): 25–42.

5 M. Lefebvre and F. Vieider, "Risk Taking of Executives Under Different Incentive Contracts: Experimental Evidence," *Journal of Economic Behaviour and Organization* 97 (2014): 27–36.

6 Margaret Yourcenar, *Memoirs of Hadrian* (2005), 214.

# 6

# STRATEGY AS PARADOX

'A thinker without paradox is like a lover without feeling: a paltry
mediocrity.'
— Soren Kierkegaard

Rosling, in his book, *Factfulness* (2018), wrote,

> Humans have a strong dramatic instinct toward binary thinking, a
> basic urge to divide things into two distinct groups, with nothing but
> an empty gap in between. But we know life is rarely like that. We love
> to dichotomize. Good versus bad. Heroes versus villains.

Most strategies are built on specific, fixed views about what is really
an unpredictable future, forcing leaders to commit to inflexible strategies
regardless of how the future might unfold. It is this commitment to a fixed
view within the reality of uncertainty that is the cause of a strategic paradox.[1] Political parties face a similar problem when they are encumbered by

DOI: 10.4324/9781003457398-7

manifesto pledges that limit their flexibility to adapt to changing conditions, although politicians don't appear to have too much of a problem breaking pledges when it suits them.

Change juxtaposes competing demands, sparking tension when the demands appear simultaneously. Humans are instinctively uncomfortable in paradoxical situations.

We can break out from the constraint of binary thinking by developing a paradoxical mindset. If we embrace paradox, rather than avoid it, and search out paradoxical problems, we can use them as a foundation to strengthen our understanding of strategic opportunities. Paradoxical problems provide an opportunity to explore issues more deeply and move from an either/or mindset to both/and optimisation.

In a paradox, we have contradictory yet interrelated elements that exist simultaneously and persist over time. A good example is the privacy paradox. There is an asymmetry between our stated privacy preferences and our actual disclosure behaviour, and this is called the privacy paradox. We say we care about privacy and profess a desire to limit the exposure of our personal information. But our observed behaviour is quite different. We share highly intimate information for meagre or no rewards. Remember that if you are not paying for the product, then you are probably the product.

The privacy paradox is only a paradox if we assume people engage in rational disclosure decision-making. Often, however, there is a misuse of design to manipulate people into disclosing data. The idea of a rational sharer is a myth. Rational choice is limited by cognition, influenced by context, and disclosure is influenced by website aesthetics and design. You can only opt out if there is an opt out button. Research groups at Princeton identified 'dark patterns in website design deceiving users into making site preferred decisions.'[2]

Let's consider the psychological aspects of dealing with paradoxical decisions and the behaviours we might expect. Behavioural psychology tells us that, when we are under pressure to make difficult decisions, we become psychologically uncomfortable. We seek to alleviate the pressure by adopting mental defences, for example, by avoiding the problem, letting someone else make the decision, going with the default option or, in the extreme, having a nervous breakdown. Corporate strategy, with its focus on decision-making, is a stressful process.

There is a theory of schizophrenia called the double bind that was first described by Gregory Bateson in the 1950s. The double bind occurs during interactions in which the individual is repeatedly exposed to conflicting injunctions without having the opportunity to respond to those injunctions. Damned if you do, damned if you don't. When you are trapped under mutually exclusive expectations, there is psychological pressure and tension. I am not suggesting that paradoxical problems can lead to schizophrenia, but the double bind concept illustrates how much psychological pressure we are under when dealing with paradoxical problems.[3]

Paul Watzlawick (1921–2007) was a psychologist, communications theorist, and a philosopher. He wrote, 'The problem isn't the problem; the problem is the way we think about the problem.' If I may slightly restate Paul Watzlawick's statement, the problem is not the tension caused by a paradoxical problem, it is how we approach the problem.

Paradoxical tensions cause anxiety and produce counterproductive defences that become vicious cycles and entrenched positions. Many of the leadership challenges we are examining in the Carillion case highlight the management team's fear of the paradoxical.

An example of a paradoxical problem is the challenge James Comey, the former head of the FBI, faced with the Hilary Clinton email issue. The FBI found over 100,000 emails on the laptop of disgraced prosecutor, Andrew Weiner. Comey had made a statement to Congress on 5 July 2016 that the Clinton investigation was closed. However, a week before the election, the FBI discovered that Andrew Weiner's laptop contained many missing emails that the FBI had not examined. The FBI has a long tradition that it does not announce matters just before an election that can impact the election. Comey was in a double bind. Should he release the fact that they were examining a new unreviewed trove of emails or wait until after the election and then potentially have to investigate or even prosecute a sitting president? It was generally assumed that Clinton would beat Trump. How did Comey deal with the paradox? Comey had a framework for dealing with challenging paradoxical decisions. He knew he would be wrong if he did or did not announce the new investigation but worked out that the cost of announcing before the election was lower than doing it after the election.

I hope a picture is starting to emerge. When you have internal tensions and behavioural dysfunction, it impacts how we think about strategy and our willingness to address challenging paradoxical issues. Leadership and leadership style become particularly important.

## Traditional Versus Paradoxical Thinking

Traditional thinking is based on the idea that there is one right answer, and we need to find it. Problems are seen as either/or – for example, us versus them – or how do we beat our rivals? Decisions are seen as a zero-sum game with a winner and a loser. The problem is exacerbated because we prefer clear, decisive leaders. We do not like uncertainty, and we see decisiveness as a strength. We mistake open-mindedness and flexibility as indecisiveness and weakness.

Strategic decisions are largely paradoxical, and we need to shift from the traditional either/or to paradoxical thinking based on both/and. How do we create strategic opportunities that fuel our efforts and encourage cooperation and experimentation by harnessing the power of paradoxical problems? Rather than one right answer in our paradoxical world, there may be multiple right answers. We need to invent and explore by shifting from a zero-sum game mindset to one based on a positive sum game, and this implies we can think about collaboration, not just competition. By adopting a leadership style that is collaborative and collective, using disciplined creativity, we can harness the power of paradox. Paradoxical thinking, however, is more challenging and takes greater self-confidence and courage.

## The Innovation Paradox

Earlier, I differentiated between incremental management based on constant improvement and strategic management, where we address larger and more fundamental issues. The core is what the organisation does today, and through our deep understanding of the core, we can use this knowledge to leverage and develop new strategies. To explore is about what we do tomorrow through investment and innovation.

Research and development (R&D) investment is a common paradoxical problem. Investing now for potential long-term gain depresses earnings, dividends, and probably the short-term share price but, if successful, strengthens the organisation for the future. Lloyds Bank for years strangled investment in retail banking technology, so their service offering fell behind the more innovative challenger banks. Perhaps the leadership at Lloyds Bank didn't think this strategic investment was important because of the lack of competition and profitability in the retail banking space and the generally abysmal level of service offered by their competitors. It is hard to estimate how much their short-term strategy damaged their reputation and future profitability, but a survey in 2021 ranked Lloyds seventh for customer satisfaction with the top five places taken by non-traditional banks.[4]

The Icarus paradox, based on a book by Danny Miller (1990), refers to the phenomenon of businesses failing abruptly after a period of apparent success and where this failure is brought about by the very elements that led to the initial success.

Did Carillion have an Icarus moment? Was the basis of Carillion's failure its unwillingness to address major problems when there was still time?

Successful business development generally follows an S curve. Firms usually start off slowly as they grow and prove their business model, and they then have a period of rapid success followed by a plateau and eventual decline. By investing at a point on the steep growth curve, you give yourself time to explore new opportunities when things are going well and there is a spirit of optimism. Addressing major problems at a point later in the cycle may be too late – for example, when the business has plateaued or is starting to decline. In Carillion's case, the growth line had collapsed into decline, but creative accounting gave the impression that the business was on a plateau. Either way, by 2015 or 2016, it was too late to turn around the company.

The duration of the S curves can be long or short, depending on the industry. In Carillion's case, it was probably five years of strong growth followed by five years of plateau and two or three years of collapse.

Strategically, it is risky to be either ahead or behind the market and market expectations. As the adage goes, 'What do pioneers get? Arrows in the back.'

## How to Address Paradoxical Problems

Smith and Lewis in their book, *Both/and Thinking* (2022), suggest that we develop a higher purpose for an organisation that is bold, clear, and consistent in order to address paradoxical problems.[5]

Management needs to move away from a zero-sum game mindset by empowering joint problem solving, actively seeking areas of agreement rather than difference, and engaging the tension of paradoxical problems.

Carillion could have dealt with their paradoxical problems with a bold position on write-downs, but the board never had the courage to address the paradoxical challenges. Maybe it was impossible for the existing management team to have won investor support in order to take the tough decisions. Perhaps with a strong new CEO, or after a takeover by a new owner, the company would have had the necessary support to change strategy.

Leading change paradoxically requires a constructive, collaborative atmosphere to draw out a team combined with the mindset of a leader who has the confidence to create an environment of non-threatening discussion and exploration. That atmosphere and leadership did not exist at Carillion.

Smith and Lewis suggest that our thinking can get stuck in a rut. They describe 'rabbit holes' where narrow patterns of choice trigger automatic responses to the same persistent problems. Another unconstructive response that they call 'wrecking balls' is when the response to a frequently encountered paradox is to make an overcorrection, pushing us into a new rut. Trench warfare is when people dig into their polarised positions.

Smith and Lewis suggest ways to move out of ruts. Using the analogy of the mule, an animal bred from a horse and an ass to bring out the best of both animals, they describe a creative approach to finding a solution to a polarised problem by integrating the poles of a paradox to move away from domination by one side. Searching for a more creative and integrated solution brings fresh and positive thinking to entranced problems. Another approach they call 'tightrope walking' uses small, careful adjustments to navigate a paradox and balance the extremes, moving forward by engaging with the conflicting demands.

The Smith and Lewis research shows that our approach to paradox is important. A paradoxical mindset starts with the assumption that multiple points of view exist and that we need to shift from the notion of controlling the challenge to one of coping with it, 'finding comfort in the discomfort to enable both/and thinking.' They outline a three-step process: first, define the underlying paradox using positive or neutral language; second, reframe the underlying problem to a both/and question; and third, find a workable solution using the mules or tightrope walkers analogies and outline a higher vision that unites the polarities. The upside and downside of each pole of the paradox should be outlined in the search for common ground with agreement on an action plan.

Building paradoxical thinking into the fabric of an organisation by using a higher purpose helps connect people to find acceptable, constructive solutions, and it avoids entrenched positions and the risk of trench warfare mentioned earlier. By encouraging low-cost experiments to test ideas before launching significant new strategies, debate is facilitated and skills are built in order to harness paradox.

A challenge is how to take an enlightened, positive approach to paradoxical challenges when the organisation is in chaos. When the factory is on fire, a manager is unlikely to focus on innovative production ideas.

## Notes

1 Michael Raynor, *The Strategy Paradox* (2007).
2 Ari Ezra Waldman, "Rational Disclosure and the Privacy Paradox," November 2019, www.behaviouraleconomics.com.
3 Mental Research Institute, Palo Alto, CA.
4 Best and Worst UK Banks for Service, February 15, 2021. City A.M.
5 Wendy Smith and Marianne Lewis, *Both/and Thinking: Embracing Creative Tensions to Solve Your Toughest Problems* (Boston: Harvard Business Review Press, 2022).

# 7

# MORAL AND ETHICAL ISSUES

Christopher Snowdon of the Institute of Economic Affairs (IEA) said, 'It is for the law to decide where salesmanship ends, and fraud begins.' And that is a good starting point for an exploration of moral issues in business.

In this section, we are going to look at moral and ethical issues and how they intertwine with organisational leadership. Continuing with our examination of Carillion, we will look at the company and its professional advisors through an ethical and corporate governance lens and consider what we can learn from the mistakes made.

I want to explore the link between corporate strategy and moral and ethical issues. Corporate strategy is about the bigger issues affecting an enterprise and its long-term direction. Many paradoxical business decisions have moral and ethical dimensions, and their prominence has increased dramatically with the pervasiveness, power, and immediacy of social media. For example, Carillion faced the issue of increasing dividend payments versus the moral obligation to ensure that the pension scheme was adequately funded. What was a fair balance between the board's responsibility to shareholders and to former employees?

DOI: 10.4324/9781003457398-8

All organisations operate in an increasingly regulated and controlled environment and are now subject to unprecedented public scrutiny through the media and social media. Our decisions as organisational leaders are tweeted, examined, ridiculed, misinterpreted, whistle-blown, and publicly aired. Slips, gaffes, and even comments at private events can become a Twitter storm or Instagram sensation within hours. The political rhetoric and negative perceptions about business are not encouraging, and we need to be aware of the ethical and moral dimensions of our strategic decisions and public optics.

In September 2022, the Financial Reporting Council (FRC) disciplinary tribunal examined allegations relating to the 2016 audit of Carillion, claiming that five respondents from the auditor KPMG created false or misleading documents. The FRC restated that a professional accountant shall comply with the fundamental principle of integrity. Professional accountants must be straightforward and honest in all professional and business relationships, and this implies fair dealing and truthfulness, and they will not knowingly be associated with reports, returns, and communications where the information contains materially false or misleading statements.

Sarah Gordon, a *Financial Times* writer for twenty years, commented on the financial crash of 2008 and the collapse of Lehman Brothers.

> This was a salutatory moment for me because it reinforced a lesson I had been learning since working in the City of London and on Wall Street in the 1990s: that the failures which led to the crisis were more of behaviour and character than of financial instruments or processes. The tales of casual greed and of ordinary people misled and deceived by irresponsible bankers and their overweening power. Business bosses who enjoy too long a tenure lose self-awareness. They become reluctant to promote people around them who will challenge their point of view. Meanwhile, questioning a boss who enjoys such stature becomes almost impossible, encouraging hubris, and leading to bad decisions.[1]

What drives leaders of organisations to behave unethically? We know from behavioural psychology that, when emotions are aroused, we behave more irrationally than we predict. Dan Ariely[2] writes, 'When there is a fear of failure or exposure of poor performance, managers will behave much more irrationally, doing things they would never do normally. This irrationality can be manifest in many ways, from poor decision-making to unethical or even illegal behaviour.' In fact, irrational behaviour is a warning sign of problems.

This is no defence, but there are numerous examples of corrupt behaviour brought about by pressure on executives to deliver strong results. Wells Fargo Bank opened an estimated 3.5 million fake customer accounts,[3] Enron defrauded states, Sackler sold opioids when they knew they were dangerously addictive, VW – one of the world's largest vehicle manufacturers – faked emissions tests, and Big Tobacco's misinformation about the health hazards from smoking is well documented. The investment bank, Goldman Sacks, pushed stocks they were shorting. Lloyds Bank peddled worthless insurance, and the LIBOR rate scandal defrauded millions of people. Despite the scale and frequency of abuse, it is very rare for executives to be tried and punished.

So, how should you address moral dilemmas? Would you propose immoral strategies that benefit your organisation, behave complicitly when they are proposed, or take a moral stand? How do you deal with the discussion of immoral or dishonest strategies? Should you remain silent or tackle the issues head-on? What are your responsibilities and legal obligations? How do you protect yourself?

Values are principles, standards, or qualities that are considered worthwhile or desirable, and they may be included in a company's mission statement. For example, American Express's 'Customer Commitment' and Google's 'Focus on the user and all else will follow.' Generally, values are neither good nor bad, they are morally relative. They need to be qualified as to how good they are or for whom they are good? Of course, good is often a matter of opinion. Carillion's vision statement said, 'We do the right thing for the customers, employees and shareholders.' It is ill-defined and does not address conflicts of interest or the paradoxes contained within it. In the end, it was shown to be meaningless.

Morals encompass the great moral values: honesty (the quality of being sincere), truth (refers to facts), freedom, charity, courage, etc. Morals are regarded as knowing the difference between right and wrong and are relative values – abstract, subjective, and often personal. You could say morals are a code of behaviour.

Honesty is a basic moral quality that is expected of all members of society. It involves being truthful about important matters. Telling lies about things that matter, or committing fraud or stealing, are generally regarded as dishonest conduct, and the legal concept of dishonesty is grounded in the shared values of society.

Integrity is a broader concept than honesty. It is a more nebulous concept and is less easy to define; however, in professional codes of conduct, it is used as a shorthand to express the higher standards that society expects from professionals.[4]

Ethics are knowing right from wrong and choosing right. Behaving ethically means having a willingness to do the right thing. Ethics are moral values and demonstrate respect for others by one's actions.

Was Carillion's dividend policy ethical? Was it morally justifiable because it was in the interest of the company's shareholders, and it reduced Carillion's borrowing costs and enhanced the share price? Or was it unethical because it benefited the directors personally, took much needed capital away from the business, and reduced funds available to meet the pension commitments made to former employees?

It is helpful to reflect on your own ethical boundaries before finding yourself in a conflicting situation. Making an ethical decision can be difficult when there are trade-offs between conflicting obligations. For example, overcharging a client who beat you up on the contract price. Lloyd's bank used this argument when they were accused of mis-selling billions of pounds of worthless insurance, claiming they had to cover the costs of all the free services they offered clients.

## Impact of an Unethical Culture

Ethics are an important dimension of corporate strategy, and an ethical strategy sets the tone for behaviour within an organisation. Unethical behaviour or dishonesty is insidious, like a tumour that spreads, and it is hard to trace and measure in an organisation.

Generally, you get the behaviour that you reward, so be careful what you reward because ill-considered rewards may encourage unethical behaviour?

There are significant hidden costs of an unethical culture that can lead to poor employee performance. An unethical culture is a stressful environment and results in increased absenteeism, health issues, and the demotivating aura of negativism. Other impacts include high employee turnover, leading to costly recruitment and training, and reduced productivity during the time taken for new employees to settle in. Other costs may include the loss of knowledge and experience, the loss of sales, and the damage to a team's morale. It is sobering to consider that the cost of staff loss is estimated to be between 50 percent to 200 percent of total salary packages. In the United States, staff turnover rates are 15 percent per year. We know that there is higher staff turnover in unethical firms, and these costs are poorly captured by traditional accounting.[5]

There is toxicity in organisations that tolerate high employee malfeasance and dishonesty. Those who cheat for you are more likely to cheat you, and their behaviour pushes away honest employees. A toxic culture will attract less honest people, and those who stay knowingly in an unethical culture are more likely to behave unethically.

Setting and maintaining a culture with high ethical standards needs to be an ongoing dimension of corporate strategy.

## The Nolan Principles 1995

In 1995, the UK government launched the Nolan Principles, seven principles guiding public life. They provide a template for any organisation, whether for profit or not, and their clarity and lack of ambiguity is refreshing. They are as follows:

1. **Selflessness:** Holders of public office should act solely in terms of the public interest.
2. **Integrity:** Holders of public office must avoid placing themselves under any obligation to people or organisations that might try inappropriately to influence them in their work. They should not act or take decisions in order to gain financial or other material benefits for themselves, their family, or their friends. They must declare and resolve any conflicting interests and relationships.
3. **Objectivity:** Holders of public office must act and take decisions impartially, fairly, and on merit, using the best evidence and without discrimination or bias.
4. **Accountability:** Holders of public office are accountable to the public for their decisions and actions and must submit themselves to the scrutiny necessary to ensure this.
5. **Openness:** Holders of public office should act and take decisions in an open and transparent manner. Information should not be withheld from the public unless there are clear and lawful reasons for so doing.

6.  **Honesty:** Holders of public office should be truthful.
7.  **Leadership:** Holders of public office should exhibit these principles in their own behaviour. They should actively promote and robustly support the principles and be willing to challenge poor behaviour wherever it occurs.

## Bystander Inaction

Why, when we see unethical behaviour, do we rarely do anything about it? Bystander inaction, a behavioural term, prevents people from speaking out or failing to take action to intervene when others are doing something wrong. We can link this idea to perceived norms, where people respond strongly to group norms. If the norm is to keep quiet, then most will follow the group norm. Courage is rare and usually punished in organisations, particularly autocratic ones. People look to others to see how to respond, especially to stronger members of the group.

Where there are issues of power imbalance, our tendency is to underestimate how hard it is for someone else to say no for fear of retribution.

How should we compensate for bystander inaction? By creating an environment that encourages people to make constructive comments. The responsibility of organisational leaders is to empower debate. Sadly, those least likely to create a constructive, empowering, and open atmosphere are autocratic or bullying leaders.

By creating structures and processes that make it easy for people to raise concerns without fear of retaliation, organisations create a more robust and positive environment where problems can be explored before they get out of control.

## Notes

1  *FT*, Weekend March 9, 2019.
2  Dan Ariely, *Predictably Irrational: The Hidden Forces That Shape Our Decisions* (New York: Harper, 2009).
3  *NPR the Two-Way*, August 31, 2017.
4  Court of Appeal. Wingate v Solicitors Regulation Society, 2018.
5  L. Branham, *Keeping the People Who Keep You in Business* (New York: American Management Association, 2000).

# 8

# CORPORATE GOVERNANCE

## Responsibilities of Directors

In Carillion's 2016 report and accounts, the company said, 'Our commitment to business integrity, safety, strong governance, and sustainability remains a key strength of our business.' In hindsight, there are clearly questions about the honesty of that statement.

Earlier, we looked at corporate governance issues and the responsibilities of company directors. The well-established law says that directors have to behave in a way that is prudent, attend to the needs of multiple stakeholders, and consider the long-term success of the enterprise. The Institute of Chartered Accountants describes the responsibility of directors as 'to facilitate effective, entrepreneurial and prudent management that can deliver long-term success of the company.' The UK Companies Act 2006 says that 'directors have a duty to promote the success of the company for the benefit of its members as a whole' and to consider 'likely consequences of a decision in the long-term' and 'act in the interest of the company's employees.' The Act goes on to say that directors should exercise reasonable care, skill, and

DOI: 10.4324/9781003457398-9

diligence. The Financial Reporting Council in its UK Corporate Governance Code states the 'underlying principles of good governance are accountability, transparency, probity and a focus on the sustainable success of an entity over the longer term.' I think that the key phrases 'long-term success' and 'sustainable success of the entity over the longer term' highlight Carillion's ultimate failure.

When a company becomes insolvent, as Carillion did, when its debts and goodwill were known to be false, the directors are breaching their duties if they continue trading and can be subject to fines and disqualification and become personally liable for wrongful trading.

## Carillion and the Auditors

In case you think that legal issues are not an important part of strategic thinking, I want to highlight some of the legal repercussions for the directors and auditors of Carillion. KPMG, Carillion's auditors, found themselves defending in the High Court a claim for damages of £1.3 billion by the Official Receiver. In February 2023, the case was settled for an undisclosed but presumably a significant amount. You will recall that just a few months after the 2016 accounts were released in March 2017, Carillion made a massive profit warning saying that sales and assets were overvalued by hundreds of millions of pounds. How could the accounts be so different within such a short time?

The role of an auditor is to obtain reasonable assurance about whether the financial statements, as a whole, are free from material misstatement.[1] If the accountants are unable to obtain sufficient appropriate audit evidence to support that assessment, they should issue a modified opinion on the accounts, noting the areas of the accounts that are the cause of that modification.

The House of Commons committees claimed that 'KPMG had been complicit in signing off on Carillion's increasingly fantastical figures' and that the internal auditor, Deloitte, had failed to identify 'terminal failings' in risk management and financial controls.[2] The House of Commons report also said that 'KPMG failed to question the dodgy accounting . . . the dysfunctional auditing industry clearly needs shaking up.'

KPMG audited Carillion for nineteen years, earning audit fees of £29 million. Michelle Hinchliffe, KPMG's Head of Audit, said she did not believe nineteen years as auditor of Carillion was 'too long to be impartial' and that 'independence for me is a mindset. For myself and all my fellow partners, independence and integrity are absolutely critical to our profession.'[3]

In KPMG's defence, they may have had limited resources to audit certain specialised elements of the accounts – for example, working out the percentage of completion of a large overseas construction project or the probability of a debt going bad. They often have no choice but to rely on the directors' estimates of the costs to complete which were estimated by divisional teams often far removed from the finance director's department.

There are two key checks that auditors should consider: revenue recognition and override of controls by management. Accounts should give a true and fair view. Auditors are engaged to give an opinion on true and fair view, not to opine on the management. Auditors can disclose Emphasis of Matter to shareholders about fundamental issues without having to qualify the accounts.

A major issue at Carillion was revenue recognition. Principally, revenue is recognised only when a critical event has occurred, and the amount of revenue is measurable. The Securities and Exchange Commission (SEC) in the United States generally uses four tests that must all be met: persuasive evidence of an arrangement exists; delivery has occurred or services have been rendered; the seller's price to the buyer is fixed or determinable; and collectability is reasonably assured.

The HoC committee said, 'Had KPMG been prepared to challenge management, the warning signs were there in highly questionable assumptions about construction contract revenue and the intangible asset of goodwill accumulated in historic acquisitions.'[4]

The Financial Reporting Council (FRC), the main regulator of company accounts, announced an inquiry into Carillion's 2014, 2015, and 2016 audits with particular focus on the company's use and disclosure of the 'going concern basis of accounting,' estimates and recognition of revenue on significant contracts, and accounting for pensions.

Given that the FRC is not a large organisation – in 2012 there were only six people at the FRC who did investigations and enforcement – it is unrealistic for them to monitor and investigate many cases to any depth. In 2019, there were only thirteen open non-audit investigations into accountants and accounting firms, and in the year 2018–2019 only fifteen cases were referred to the Conduct Committee. In the case of the lender, Cattles plc that collapsed in 2009 losing £1 billion of shareholders' funds, it took the FRC seven years to finally reprimand the auditors. The FRC has a staff of about 200 and a budget of £60 million which is a minnow compared to the Financial Conduct Authority (FCA) with 3,700 staff and a £600 million budget.

The role of Carillion's Audit Committee certainly needs examination. The FRC, in its guidance to members of the audit committee of a public company, says, 'The audit committee has a particular role, acting independently from the executive, to ensure that the interests of shareholders are properly protected in relation to financial reporting and internal control.' Clearly, Carillion's audit committee failed to properly protect shareholders and all of the other stakeholders.[5]

Carillion recognised considerable amounts of construction revenue that was traded and not certified. This was revenue that clients had not yet signed off on such as for claims and variations and, therefore, it was inherently uncertain whether payment would be received. In December 2016, the company was recognising £294 million of traded but not certified revenue, an increase of over £60 million since June 2014 and accounting for over 10 percent of total revenue from construction contracts. The amount of revenue that was traded but not certified was never publicly disclosed in financial statements but was included in papers reviewed quarterly by the audit committee.

The Carillion Finance Director, Zafar Khan who signed off the 2016 accounts, said he did 'not agree that there was a concerted effort to adopt aggressive accounting as such' and that the numbers reported 'were appropriate, based on the information that was available at that point in time.' As part of a contract review that led to the July 2017 provision, management were asked by KPMG to consider whether the results indicated that the 2016 accounts had been misstated due to either fraud or error. The position the board chose to adopt publicly was that there was no misstatement and that the provisions all related to the sudden deterioration of positions on key contracts between March and June 2017.[6]

An experienced senior executive from the construction industry told me,

> There is a significant industry issue within this part of the debate in that fair, reasonable and prudent, value/revenue is often not certified during live construction contracts, and the contract form chosen also has an impact. In many industries, cash received provides a reasonable trading position or benchmark. Often in construction, cash is received ahead of true earned value, and trading cash receipts, can sometimes lead to overstatement of revenue.

The construction industry executive added, 'In my view, companies should have to report uncertified value, but it is the trend that would be more telling than the fact it exists.'

Company accounts are part of the transparency process. Are they transparent enough? Do they show an honest picture? What are the biases and conflicts of interest that affect honest reporting?

There is a risk of strategic decisions being driven by disclosure and measurement pressures, a problem that affects many organisations, particularly public services such as the National Health Service, the police, and universities. Does increased transparency make us more honest, or does it encourage gaming the system to meet the stated targets? These are challenging questions to answer.

## Carillion and the Fallout for Auditors and Directors

The House of Commons MP Frank Field, who served on the Work and Pensions Committee, said of the Carillion directors, 'stuffing their mouths with gold while their companies go to rack and ruin with thousands thrown out of work and pension schemes impoverished. There is a word for people who appropriate other people's money: thief.'[7]

Scapegoats? Anti-business rhetoric? Oversimplification? Fair comment? Is this left-wing polemic and political grandstanding? Is it part of the 'all businessmen are greedy fat-cats?' Or is it a distorted description of a team that built a large international business while completing many significant construction contracts and paying millions in UK tax revenue but eventually failing to sustain the business through mismanagement?

The former CEO, Richard Howson, testified to the Select Committee that 'the business was in a sustainable position.' But, as we know the end of the story, that was clearly wrong. Were the seeds of failure already sown when the company took over Mowlem and McAlpine a decade earlier? Under insolvency law, a director may be guilty of wrongful trading if they knew, or ought to have known, that there was no realistic prospect of a company avoiding liquidation or administration.

The Carillion case raises many interesting questions. Was everyone on the board guilty? What about the next level of senior management? What about auditors and other professional advisors? Did the Report and Accounts achieve their objectives of disclosure and clear reporting of risk?

The Carillion story will run for many years and numerous official investigations are ongoing, including: The Insolvency Service, Financial Reporting Council, Financial Conduct Authority, The Pensions Regulator, The National Audit Office, The Public Accounts Committee, The Public Administration, The Constitutional Affairs Committee, and a separate report by the National Audit Office (NAO) on Whitehall's handling of Carillion PFI hospital contracts.

In a February 2019 *Financial Times* report,[8] Madison Marriage wrote, 'The accounting industry and its four largest companies – EY, PwC, Deloitte, and KPMG – have been hit by scandal after scandal, which have called into question the quality of their audit work . . . criticism of the industry has been relentless, and regulators are assessing whether to break up the Big Four or impose other reforms. One suggestion is a clawback of audit fees if a client firm goes bust.'

The FCA has investigated allegations of insider trading at Carillion. The FCA chief at the time, Andrew Bailey who later became the Governor of the Bank of England, said he was looking into allegations that people connected to the company had traded in its shares using inside knowledge before Carillion's huge profit warning on 10 July 2017. The FCA announced in January 2019 that it would investigate concerns that Carillion had manipulated financial statements in the years before it collapsed. Bailey said, 'Our investigation is into the timeliness and content of the firm's announcements. Our primary focus is to determine whether the matters announced in Carillion's trading update on 10 July 2017 were identified and announced at the appropriate time.'

Calls for the breakup of the big four accounting firms have increased, and the Competition and Markets Authority (CMA) recommended that the government pass new laws forcing accounting giants to put greater distance between the audit divisions and their more lucrative consulting operations in order to prevent conflicts of interest. The regulator considered that a quarter of big company audits were substandard.[9]

The problems for KPMG, Carillion's auditors, have become more complex and dangerous. KPMG signed unqualified audit reports in the financial statements from their appointment in 1999 to the last set of audited accounts in 2016, and they declared the company was a going concern even in the last interim results published in July 2017. The firm now faces significant negligence lawsuits brought by the British government's liquidators, the

Insolvency Service. One suit for £250 million relates to Carillion's payout of dividends of £234.2 million and consultancy fees of £17 million between 2014 and 2016, and it claims that KPMG were negligent in its accounting for goodwill.

In July 2017, Carillion wrote down contracts valued at £845 million and wrote off £134 million in goodwill. Two contracts alone, Battersea Power Station and the Msheireb project in Qatar, were overstated by £352 million.[10]

In January 2022, the Chief Executive of KPMG apologised for misconduct in misleading the UK accounting regulator, the FRC, and admitted to fabricating documents and the minutes of meetings. The FRC allege that KPMG's Richard Kitchen edited the formula on a spreadsheet to increase the threshold for scrutiny of contracts from £300,000 to £1.5 million – and KPMG have already admitted this misconduct.

In February 2022, KPMG faced a £1.3 billion claim in an unprecedented action by the Insolvency Receiver as it tries to maximise returns for creditors, including the UK government. Filed in the High Court, the massive claim is for audit negligence and includes the initial claim of over £200 million for dividends paid out. A spokesperson for the receiver said,

> Following extensive investigations looking into the causes of Carillion's liquidation, the official receiver has submitted a claim to the High Court concerning KPMG's role as auditor for the company's accounts. The official receiver has taken this action in the interests of creditors who lost substantially in the liquidation. The decision is based on legal advice, which is that KPMG is answerable to Carillion's creditors for losses that have been caused.

The official receiver claims that KPMG missed red flags that the accounts were misstated and that the group was insolvent more than two years before it collapsed. Previous court documents showed the claim was expected to be in the region of £250 million. Recent court judgements, however, had redrawn the test for professional negligence.

The Carillion directors also face litigation. Eight former Carillion directors, denied wrongdoing and are defending a separate legal action by the Insolvency Service which is seeking to ban them from running UK companies. In 2023 Adams was banned from being a director for 11 years. In July 2022, the Financial Conduct Authority provisionally fined former Carillion chief executive, Richard Howson, and former finance directors, Richard Adam and Zafar Khan, a total of £870,200 over three misleadingly positive statements between December 2016 and May 2017. The FCA said it considered that Howson, Adam, and Khan 'acted recklessly and were knowingly concerned in Carillion's contraventions.' The FCA said the three executives,

> were each aware of the deteriorating expected financial performance within Carillion's UK construction business and the increasing finan-cial risks associated with it. They failed to ensure that those Carillion announcements for which they were responsible accurately and fully reflected these matters.[11]

## Legal Governance and Political Pressure

We should be aware of the historical context when reviewing past events. Changes in government policy and direction impact how we make deci-sions at one point in time, and they can appear wrong in a different political environment.

The Pensions Regulator was under pressure from the government to be more business-friendly between 2011 and 2014, when Carillion faced pleas to put more money into the pension scheme.

Mark Boyle, non-exec chairman of the board of the regulator, said, 'There was increasing clamour to support corporate growth . . . the Treasury was particularly vocal.'

According to the Institute for Government's (IfG's) report in March 2020 about the Carillion collapse, the government contributed to creating a 'cor-porate monster' by inviting companies to bid for low-margin, high-risk pro-jects. The government offloaded too much risk onto private-sector suppliers as a result of careless outsourcing. The IfG report claimed that the cost to the taxpayer of letting Carillion collapse was about £62 million. However, this seems like a ridiculously low figure when adding in the cost of the pension bailout, the loss of tax revenue, the cost of the collapse of many small busi-nesses, and the vast sums required to complete public contracts including two major hospitals.

The IfG report described the Carillion collapse as a 'stark illustration of a rotten corporate culture' that took big debt-fuelled risks and used aggres-sive accounting to hide its problems. There will always be an impossible balancing act between getting the best value for taxpayers' money and not squeezing contractors so hard that they cannot survive.

The last chapters of this book cover a wide range of issues – from biases, hubris, and wilful ignorance to ideas about risk and the challenge and opportunity of addressing paradoxical problems.

Organisations are increasingly held accountable to a wider audience through social media. Decisions that are agreed upon quietly in the boardroom can be rapidly magnified into crisis problems if they become newsworthy or have a sensational twist. Accountability will increase, and our strategic decisions need to be based on defensible strategies that consider an ever-broadening group of stakeholders.

I want to pose some questions for further reflection on the Carillion saga in the later chapters. Could or should the scale of Carillion's problems have been detected earlier? What action could the directors have taken to mitigate the risks, and did they compound the problems because of their actions or inaction? When was it too late to save the company, and was there a watershed moment when collapse was inevitable? What lessons about decision-making and leadership can we apply from the Carillion story? Finally, although the collapse of the company impacted many stakeholders, is this the price that we pay for a free-market economy?

## Notes

1  HoC 353.
2  Guardian and Select Committee Report, May 16, 2018.
3  HoC p51 para 116.357.
4  Ibid., 769.
5  FRC Guidance on Audit Committees 2012.
6  HoC 303–5.
7  Ibid., 769.
8  *FT*, February 22, 2019. Time to rebuild flimsy foundations of accountancy.
9  *Reuters*, April 2, 2019. UK lawmakers want Big Four accounting firms broken up.
10  *Building*, November 29, 2022.
11  *FT*, July 28, 2022, Mark Wembridge and Michael O'Dwyer.

# 9

## STRATEGIC TOOLKIT

Reasoning is the action of thinking about something in a logical and sensible way, and it is a key part of decision-making. Decision-making is about the choice of actions, and reasoning is how we explain the choice to ourselves and others.

The great American businessman and long-time CEO of General Motors, Alfred P. Sloan, said,

> Gentlemen, I take it we are all in complete agreement on the decision here. Then, I propose we postpone further discussion of this matter until the next meeting to give ourselves time to develop disagreement, and perhaps gain some understanding of what the decision is all about.

Sloan added, 'I never give orders, I sell my ideas to my associates if I can . . . I prefer to appeal to the intelligence of a man rather than attempt to exercise authority over him.'

DOI: 10.4324/9781003457398-10

Jeff Bezos, the founder of Amazon said, 'When the anecdotes and the data disagree, the anecdotes are usually right.'

We have explored the challenges facing decision-makers and how these challenges affect strategic choices. We have looked at risk, biases, and behavioural flaws, and we have examined how they affect the way we think and act. We now have a better understanding of the power of paradoxical decisions and how they can be harnessed in a positive way to tackle strategic challenges.

Let's now move on to examine a range of models that can be used as tools to enhance our decision-making. I've called this section a toolkit. Armed with a range of tools, and an understanding of how they can be used, enables us to refine our decision-making abilities and hopefully reduce more obvious errors. However, each situation is unique with its own dynamics, and there are rarely clearly right or wrong answers. Often, good decisions work out badly, and bad decisions sometimes work out well. Luck, good and bad, plays its part as the author, Jerome K. Jerome, wisely observed: 'Life will always remain a gamble, with prizes sometimes for the imprudent, and blanks so often to the wise.'

When a plumber comes to your kitchen with a large box of tools, he looks at the problem and selects the right tool. But what if the plumber was an economist or politician and did plumbing in their spare time? What if the expert came with one tool and then looked for a problem that could be solved with that tool? You would be happier and more confident with the person who had a large toolbox and who would diagnose the problem first and then use the most appropriate tools to solve it. The test of any decision-making model is if it is useful for making better decisions in our world of uncertainty.

## Problem Solving and Puzzles Versus Mysteries

Earlier, I mentioned that there is a difference between a puzzle and a mystery. To recap, a puzzle has a solution – for example, a jigsaw or an equation – and we just need to work it out to find the answer and solve the problem. A mystery, however, is subtly different because mysteries don't have one solution. Most strategic problems are mysteries.

Puzzles, to use Malcolm Gladwell's definition, are 'transmitter-dependent.' They turn on what we are told. Puzzles can be solved with accurate and sufficient information. Mysteries are 'receiver-dependent.' They turn on the skill of the listener and can be distorted by noise from, for example, too much data.

A mystery cannot be solved. Reasoning through mysteries requires us to acknowledge ambiguities and resolve them sufficiently to clarify our thinking. A mystery must first be framed, well or badly, to help people make decisions in an environment of uncertainty. Framing begins by identifying critical factors and assembling relevant data. We must accept an element of luck, and we should build resilience into our decision models so that they are both strong and flexible to meet the unknown.

## Big Picture Audit

Richard Rumelt in *Good Strategy/Bad Strategy* (2011) recommended asking an important question, 'What's going on here?' A great deal of strategy work is trying to figure out what is going on. Not just deciding what to do but the more fundamental problem of comprehending the situation.

A useful exercise is to write a one-page document identifying key ideas, issues, and assumptions, together with comments on their robustness. This process of adopting a helicopter perspective aids in the comprehension of the big picture, getting down to what really matters. From this exercise, you can draw out the elements that are important to get right, what mistakes must you avoid, and confirm that your confidence is based on facts and not wishful thinking or coloured by the urgencies of the moment.

When thinking about the big picture, behave like a detective, looking for clues and finding information. All this takes time and diligence, and the risk of making mistakes increases when there is pressure either to make a decision or to get back to managing current challenges. As Daniel Kahneman pointed out, time pressure pushes us to apply fast Type 1 thinking instead of slowing down and switching to more thoughtful Type 2 thinking. Ask yourself, is the thinking time commensurate with the risk and danger of unintended consequences?

Some years ago, we were involved in the acquisition of a large leisure complex in Canada. The due diligence from accounting and legal perspectives was intense and expensive. Our team was experienced but failed to analyse properly a critically important piece of information. The cost of construction at the complex was extremely low, and we mistakenly thought this was because of lower material and labour costs. But it wasn't. It was a red-flag warning. The numbers were wrong and indicated the opposite of our conclusion about lower costs. The real cause was deep-rooted problems of misrepresentation. Perhaps, if we had been under less time pressure and had taken a step back, we might have avoided a lengthy and expensive strategic mistake.

There is an advantage in asking the dumb questions and listening carefully to the answers. It is a form of stress testing decisions. Powerful questions such as how do you know, how are you so confident in your view, or why does this strategy make sense teases out the underlying assumptions. As every subordinate knows, however, asking these sorts of questions takes courage and confidence. Good leaders are comfortable with these searching questions, and they respect the probing of assumptions and don't see them as a threat to their authority. However, those who rule by fear and diktat and/or are plagued with insecurity will no doubt bite back with aggression, attempted humiliation, and even dismissal. One diplomatic workaround is to ask a working group to ask the questions and then present their summary to the key decision-maker.

When you are part of a team addressing strategic issues, being aware of behavioural factors such as biases provides a powerful and often fresh perspective. The key point is that making better decisions takes time and cognitive effort, both of which are scarce resources.

## Auditing the Organisation's Culture

Understanding an organisation's culture creates a foundation for approaching the challenges of strategic decisions. In order to do that, identify the leadership style. Is it bold, brave, and action oriented, with or without a plan? Or is it cautious and careful with a clear road map? Are leaders consultative and patient or dictatorial and impatient? What is driving the CEO or key decision-maker? Where are they in their careers? For example, early or late stage? Are they making or defending a reputation, how have they behaved towards risk in the past? Who are the important stakeholders? What are their objectives, time frames, and styles?

The UK GEC company was one of Europe's most successful engineering and defence groups with a turnover in 1996 of £11 billion and over £1 billion in cash on its conservative balance sheet. GEC was one of Britain's most profitable companies. It ran with a lean head office of 130 people. Phillips Electronics, who was of similar size, had a head office with 14,000 staff. GEC's model was based on central financial management with strict budgetary control from the centre but loose central management of operational decisions. Strategic decisions were left to the autonomous businesses. When the founder, Lord Arnold Weinstock, stepped down in 1996, he appointed a new CEO with a very different focus and style. The new strategy was a disaster, and after three years of aggressive diversification and acquisitions, the company was wiped out.

As you deepen your understanding of an organisation, reflect on the internal and external pressures, the time horizons, stakeholder expectations (which are likely to be paradoxical), and the competitive pressures of the marketplace. What are the major concerns, hopes, and fears, and how is the organisation addressing them? The clearer the picture of culture and values, the greater your sense of what needs to be addressed and what might be achievable.

Identify networks and power, both formal and informal. Who is really in charge? As the adage goes, it is not who sits on the throne – it's who pulls the strings. In Carillion's case, it seems that the power of the finance director, Richard Adam, far exceeded that of the CEO, the chairman, and the rest of the board – not officially, but in practice.

There is an increasing sense of idealism, especially among younger people. Failure to acknowledge these idealistic viewpoints can lead to employee disillusion and demotivation. However, getting things done demands a practical and pragmatic approach, and steering through paradoxes such as profit versus social responsibility requires sensitivity, nuanced communication, and careful implementation.

## Warning Signs

Fund manager, Tim Steer, wrote *The Signs Were There* in 2018, and it is an insightful workbook that points to numerous signs that a company is in trouble. By considering Steer's checklist, we can see warning signs that were present in the Carillion story long before the collapse. These signs are important, too, as they impact the underlying assumptions for strategic decisions. 'If the accounting information is flawed, then we have a false foundation for making key decisions.' This was the case at Carillion, where off-balance-sheet borrowing distorted the cash flow problems, overvalued receivables greatly exaggerated the profits, and worthless goodwill overstated the assets of the business.

Steer's red flags include a reliance on acquisitions to keep profits moving, large and seemingly unsubstantiated goodwill, too optimistic debt recovery and growing accrued income, and repeated worrying trends in performance. One of the leading reasons for going bust is poor cash flow and that is exactly what happened at Carillion. In fact, all these factors are dominant in the Carillion story.

Acquisitive companies rarely add shareholder value.

> Marriages between companies start off with good intentions but rarely do they turn out the way management expected them to. Acquisitive companies often fail to deliver shareholder value and in general it is wise to avoid those that seem to be addicted to growth through acquisition.

A study in the United States by the Big Four accounting firm, Deloitte, showed that only a quarter of merger or acquisition deals deliver enhanced value. That was certainly the case for several of Carillion's major acquisitions.

Reliance on acquisitions for growth, according to Steer, is a warning sign. It is only a matter of time before acquisitions usually unravel. From a strategic perspective, it is important to understand if the organisation truly has the management depth, experience, and bandwidth to deal with the complex process of post-acquisition integration. Rarely do the expected synergies work out.

Accrued income is the income that a company says it has earned but has not yet invoiced the customer, and neither has it received the cash. Accrued income is recognised in the period that it has been earned and not in the period the cash is received. Large amounts of accrued income is a warning sign because a firm may be waiting a long time for the income or may never receive it, leading to cash flow problems. This was a serious issue for Carillion. When their accrued income was shown to be false, it had a dramatic impact on profits and management's credibility. It is unlikely that a leadership team can make rational strategic decisions at a time of significant profit warnings.

Carillion was one of the most shorted UK stocks in 2016. Short selling a stock indicates serious concerns about the future performance of the company. It means that sophisticated investors predict that a share price is going to fall significantly, and it is a clear indicator of a lack of confidence in the business's future.

A useful tip is to read annual reports from back to front because the front tends to have glossy pictures and upbeat statements, whereas the back contains more hard facts and details. Carillion's accounts were over 180 pages long, and it takes time and attention to spot signs of trouble that are often buried in the details. An auditor will focus on solvency issues to test whether a firm can meet its long-term commitments. However, auditors are watchdogs, not bloodhounds, and the grey areas of accounting, as we learned from Carillion, leave management with significant flexibility to distort the numbers.

If you are part of a strategic team, it is important to be familiar with the information in the report and accounts. That provides financial and risk data that might not be internally disseminated to senior management below the board. Creating a strategic plan that is at variance with the publicly stated aims of the organisation, or based on significantly false information, is unlikely to be successful.

## Decision-making Models

Yale professor, Victor Vroom, identified five types of decision-making processes, each varying in degree of participation by the leader. It is helpful to understand your own approach to leadership and decision-making and that you find what style works most effectively for you and your team.

Let's look at Vroom's types of decision-making processes and leadership types:

**Decide:** The leader makes the decision or solves the problem alone and announces his or her decision to the group. The leader may gather information from members of the group. In the extreme, 'When I want your opinion, I will tell you what it is!'

**Consult individually:** The leader approaches group members individually and presents them with a problem. The leader records the suggestions and decides whether or not to use the information provided by group members.

**Consult group:** The leader holds a group meeting where he or she presents the problem to the group. All members are asked to contribute and make suggestions during the meeting. The leader makes his or her decision alone, choosing which information obtained from the group meeting to use or discard.

**Facilitate:** The leader holds a group meeting where he or she presents a problem to the group. This differs from the consult approach as the leader ensures that his or her opinions are not given any more weight than those of the group. The decision is made by group consensus and not solely by the leader.

**Delegate:** The leader does not actively participate in the decision-making process. Instead, the leader provides resources – for example, information about a problem, and encouragement is offered. Remember that there is a significant difference between delegating and abdicating. Vroom identified seven situational factors that leaders should consider when choosing a decision-making process:

**Decision significance:** How will a decision affect a project's success or the organisation as a whole?

**Importance of commitment:** Is it important that team members are committed to the final decision?

**Leader's expertise:** How knowledgeable is the leader regarding the problem(s) at hand?

**Likelihood of commitment:** If the leader makes a decision, how committed would the group members be to the decision?

**Group support for objectives:** To what degree do group members support the objectives of the leader and the organisation?

**Group expertise:** How knowledgeable are the group members regarding the problem(s) at hand?

**Team competence:** How well can group members work together to solve a problem?

Vroom created several matrices that allow leaders to take into consideration these seven situational influences in order to choose the most effective decision-making process.

## Gary Klein on Decision-making

Gary Klein is an American psychologist. He describes the reality of decision-making in complex situations that require a workable solution rather than a process of optimisation.

Klein found that experienced decision-makers assess a situation and judge it based on familiarity with a similar decision and not on comparing options. Courses of action can be quickly evaluated by mentioning how they will be carried out, not by formal analysis and comparison. Decision-makers usually look for the first workable option they can find, not the best option. Since the first action they consider is usually workable, they do not generate a large set of options to be sure they get a good one. They generate and evaluate options one at a time, and they do not bother comparing the advantages and disadvantages of alternatives.

In his book, *Seeing What Others Don't* (2013), Klein suggests conducting a 'pre-mortem' by anticipating what will go wrong, working back to discover why, and then working through how you can reduce the risk. It is clearly important to think about the costs if you are wrong, and any attempt to quantify these will be better than ignoring the question.

Unfortunately, we are not good at thinking about worst-case scenarios. We don't like to be negative when the group is positive, and holding back other people's enthusiasm is perceived as a negative characteristic.

The challenge of exploring a worst-case outcome is a common problem with acquisitions. Everybody is excited about a deal, they have worked long and hard to make it happen, often significant costs have been racked up, and it is very difficult to walk away from a deal when you are significantly invested both financially and emotionally in the transaction going ahead.

One effective strategy is to agree on the rules up front for stopping or quitting and writing them down. Another is discussing and defining what winning means for different groups. Often winning is not about money. Interestingly, professional poker players quit their hands about 80 percent of the time compared to amateurs who only do so 50 percent of the time. Presumably, the professionals have greater control of their biases.

Probabilistic thinking is essentially trying to estimate the likelihood of an outcome happening by using tools of statistics and logic. It is important to develop this skill to avoid worrying about highly improbable events and to raise awareness and plan for those that have a higher probability. Thinking probabilistically helps ground our decision-making. The process of thinking through a likelihood of something occurring is always helpful, and it moves us away from the subjective to the objective.

## Rational Thinking Process

Before looking at some models of the rational thinking process, I want to clarify what rational thinking is. Let me add that rational thinking should not be confused with the rational economic model that we discussed at the beginning of the book.

In the Great War of 1914, each belligerent government convinced itself it was acting rationally. How do we convince ourselves that we are acting rationally, and what do we understand by being rational?

Cynthia Richetti and B. B. Tregoe came up with a clear definition of rational thinking: 'Rational thinking is the ability to consider the relevant variables of a situation and to access, organize and analyse relevant information including facts, opinions, judgments, and data, to arrive at a sound conclusion.'[1] Kay and King expand this definition, suggesting that:

> Rational thinking in ordinary usage suggests two characteristics of rational judgment or action. First, the judgment or action would be based on beliefs about the world which were reasonable. Second the judgments should have internal logic or consistency and that the judgment or action is appropriate given the beliefs about the world which give rise to it.[2]

There are many models of the rational thinking process. Common elements look first at inputs and content – including experience, opinions, facts, and data – and stress the importance of accurate information from the right people. Second is the process of rational thinking based on analysis of the information. Third is the output based on sound conclusions. Content is an essential and important part of the rational thinking process. However, as we have discussed in earlier chapters, the input phase is subject to bias, self-interest, selective interpretation, misrepresentation, framing, and a host of other factors that can derail us from making rational decisions.

In the processing of inputs, how do we define our decision-making criteria? How do we weight the risks of wrong decisions and put a price on those risks? Complex issues usually involve multiple concerns, viewpoints, and tangents. Emotions are involved, stakeholders have different agendas that may be competing, and all this is in an environment of uncertainty.

Dr. Sabrina Rachel Cohen-Hatton is a remarkable person. She is a British firefighter who joined the fire service as an eighteen-year-old and who had spent time as a homeless person, surviving by selling copies of The Big Issue. Cohen-Hatton rose through the ranks of the fire service, took time out to complete her Ph.D. on decision-making under pressure, and published a bestselling book, *The Heat of the Moment* (2019).

Dr. Cohen-Hatton says, 'Decision-making is a learned skill; leadership, decision-making, situational awareness, and communication are not instinctive abilities. They are acquired with practice and hard work.'[3] She found that commanders make decisions based on the 'right now' rather than the 'what will be.' The decision-controls checklist she developed helps to shift right now to what will be. Her five-step checklist could well be applied to many organisational strategic decisions:

1.  Why are we doing this? What are the goals linked to this decision?
2.  What is the rationale, and is it jointly agreed? Does it support working together, saving lives, and reducing harm?
3.  What do we think will happen? What is the likely outcome of the action; in particular, what is the impact on the objective and other activities?
4.  How will the incident change as a result of these actions? What outcomes do we expect?
5.  In the light of these considerations, is the benefit proportional to the risk?

Do the benefits of the proposed actions justify the risks that would be accepted? Do we have a common understanding and position on the situation, its likely consequences, and potential outcomes? What is the available information, the critical uncertainties, and the key assumptions? What terminology and measures are being used by all those involved in the response? What are the individual agency working practices related to a joint response? What conclusions have been drawn and communications made? As an individual, is the collective decision in line with my professional judgement and experience? Are we, as individuals and as a team, content that this decision is the best practice solution?

Cohen-Hatton's model is a clear and structured approach that can easily be adapted to test any important decision and has the advantage of forcing the decision-makers to clarify their goals and be open about their expectations.

## Dealing With Thinking and Reasoning Errors

What are the characteristics of poor decision-makers? Kay and King suggest,

> Victims of ideology or arrogance, often talking more than listening, failing to acknowledge that on almost any subject someone knows more than they do, they believe themselves capable of ranking all possible uncertain bets – ready to swing on every pitch.

In contrast, 'Good decision-makers listen respectfully, and range widely to seek relevant advice and facts before they form a preliminary view. And when they arrive at that view, they invite challenge to it before drawing the discussion to a conclusion.' They tend to be 'More open-minded people, who look for evidence to contradict their views and are much better at rational decision-making. Most importantly, they demonstrate curiosity.'[4]

In an earlier chapter, we considered motivated reasoning when people with strong convictions, and finding contrary evidence, work harder to rationalise their beliefs. People who are more intelligent are better at coming up with rationalisations rather than changing their positions, and this is a problem for them. Being aware of the trap of motivated reasoning is helpful in order to mitigate it. Remember, intelligence and wisdom are not the same thing.[5]

How might we deal with thinking and reasoning errors without alienating colleagues? When we make direct challenges to people's thinking, they will naturally become more defensive and entrenched, particularly when they are under pressure. There are many ways to manage the process of tackling challenging decisions and reducing the risk of backlash. Asking for more details and how their proposal will work encourages positive reflection on issues. If you are presenting your proposal, offering better explanations with more reasons for something makes your story or narrative more compelling. For example, the statement, 'He was charged but cleared of corruption, he resigned,' could be modified by adding, 'He was offered an important new position.' The addition takes away the feeling that the reason he left was the corruption charge. The first sentence left the outcome to the imagination of the reader who was primed by the word, corruption, to jump to an inference about why the person resigned.

Issues are often linked to other issues in people's minds even if they are not, in fact, connected. For example, climate change has been linked to free trade or globalisation. So, attacking one issue might be seen as attacking all of someone's positions and unrelated issues. It is better to disentangle issues up front, and reframing the issue can help.

By appealing to an alternative identity, perhaps using subtle flattery or empathy can cool a situation when emotions for or against a decision can be running high. By persuading people to take an outsider's perspective, and encouraging a more detached mindset, an increase in psychological distance from a problem is often created. For example, asking how another part of an organisation or a competitor might see a decision. It is certainly true that being polite, showing respect and consideration, are more likely to help your arguments than trying to signal your own superiority.

## Importance of Narrative

Daniel Kahneman said, 'No one ever made a decision because of a number. They need a story. The power of narrative . . . rests on the capacity to help us make sense of a complex and confusing world.'

When thinking about strategic challenges, the narrative, or the story about what is going on here, needs to be clear and realistic. Narrative reasoning is a powerful tool for organising imperfect knowledge in addition to being a strategic thinking tool. You can improve your understanding of an organisation and significant issues by working on the narrative.

Higher skilled decision-makers tend to be good listeners. They are attentive to a narrative as a foundation for their decisions and, at the same time, sensitive to the possibility that a narrative may be neat but false. This willingness to challenge the prevailing narrative appears to be a key element in good decision-making.

Economist and Nobel laureate, Robert Schiller, sees narratives as fads and a departure from the rational because they do not optimise behaviour, and he points out that narratives are often dishonest and manipulative. 'The value of challenging the narrative is not simply to find out what is going on, it is to test the weakness of the proposed plan of action, to secure robustness and resilience.' Risk-averse leaders are reluctant to move outside the comfort zone of the established narrative.

In contrast, risk-takers are constantly searching for new narratives. Elon Musk is a classic example. This constant search for a new narrative can make for a wild ride, but when you pull it off, there is the biggest payback.

However, remember survivor bias. For every Steve Jobs or Elon Musk, there are thousands, perhaps tens of thousands, of entrepreneurial visionaries with engaging narratives who have failed.

## Decision Analysis Models

There are numerous models for assisting with making decisions. Richetti and Sherrin offer an example of one structured approach. A model is only a tool for keeping your thinking disciplined, and it is not a guarantee of success or even of making good decisions. But any approach that slows down the process so that we think carefully, reflect deeply on the options, and manage our personal biases will be a benefit. Richetti and Sherrin use a series of acronyms to take you through the process:

SELECT is the first stage of the process. This involves state the decision that needs to be made, establish and classify the objectives, list the alternatives, evaluate the alternatives, consider the risk, trust your work, and pick a winner.

The next step is called Complex Scenarios and Situation Appraisal and uses the acronym, SCAN, for see the issues, clarify the issues, assess the priorities, and name the next steps.

Stage three is addressing the problems and uses the acronym, PLAN, for predict potential problems, list the causes of problems, agree on preventive actions, and note the contingent actions.

The last step in Richetti's model is to determine the best action. The acronym is FIND and stands for focus on the problems, identify what is and is not a problem to avoid the allure of the deceptively simple and watch out for simple solutions to complex problems, narrow the possible causes and, finally, if you are not completely exhausted by these endless acronyms, determine the true course.[6]

Let me briefly introduce the DACI decision-making framework that is designed to improve a team's effectiveness and velocity on projects. DACI, an acronym for Driver (the project leader), Approver (person who has the final say), Contributions (the people who contribute), and Informed (the people who aren't directly involved in the decision but who need to be informed). Team members are assigned specific roles and responsibilities when it comes to group decisions. Projects are broken down into tasks but without timelines during the initial stage, and the objective is to agree on action items and prioritise them. Approvers and contributors are then assigned to each task, and they then define the actual workflow.[7]

I am not suggesting that Richetti's approach or the DACI models are uniquely useful, but they give you a flavour of the many models that are available to bring structure to decision-making. Different approaches to decision-making have a common theme. They push you to slow down, evaluate the options, think things through in a logical and disciplined manner, and reach a more reasoned judgement. What is important is using a model rather than just winging it.

## Herbert Simon and Administrative Behaviour

'The Problem of choice is one of describing consequences.'

Herbert Simon

I wrote about Herbert Simon earlier in this book. Simon developed a model for identifying stages in decision-making, and he wrote,

> The division of the decision-making process into such subprocesses as: 1) setting the agenda; 2) representing the problem; 3) finding alternatives; and 4) selecting alternatives has sometimes been criticized as describing decision-making falsely as a linear process and thereby rigidifying it.

Simon states that there is nothing linear about the decision-making process, and this brings us full circle to what we learned when we examined the limitations of the traditional model used for strategic planning. Simon states that self-evidently we want well-structured problems, goal tests that are clear and easily applied, and there needs to be a structured process for analysing potential solutions. He adds that the power of analysis depends on expert knowledge for its speed and effectiveness. In addition, he highlights the role of intuition and judgement and links this both to experience and the realities of time constraints. 'The experienced manager has in his memory a large amount of knowledge gained from experience and training, and it is organized in terms of recognizable chunks and associated information.'[8]

When developing strategy, a vital starting point is setting an agenda so that priorities are addressed logically and proportionately. There must be a process for setting and revising an agenda, and Herbert Simon suggests that all that is required is a simple mechanism that will signal priorities. As signals gradually increase in intensity, priorities will emerge. This approach allows us to avoid thinking about maximisation. Simon suggests that this crude procedure will work satisfactorily, not optimally, if there is time to carry out searches to generate solutions before problems become critical.

What priorities were Carillion signalling? And how were they dealing with the signals? Were those strategic risks minimised, their signals distorted, because management didn't want to address them?

Simon points out that problems are items that, if not attended to, will cause trouble. In contrast, opportunities are items that, if attended to, may increase profits or even impact the probability of surviving. Until they are noticed, opportunities are not opportunities. A great many of them, including those of the first order of magnitude, secure their place on an agenda through informed surprise.

An interesting example of both an opportunity and a problem faced Hays Travel in 2019. The Thomas Cook travel agency collapsed, creating an opportunity for the family-run Hays Travel to triple the size of their outlets with the acquisition of Thomas Cook's 555 branches and with adding 2,300 staff to the Sunderland-based company. It was a curious decision because on-line travel booking was replacing traditional retail travel agent outlets. It was a challenging and exciting opportunity for Hays, but the timing couldn't have been worse. Less than six months later, the Covid lockdowns started, and international travel and non-essential retail shops were closed. Following dramatic steps to reduce costs, culminating in cutting over 500 jobs and closing all non-essential shops, Hays weathered the storm better than most competitors because of their prompt action and from help with generous government programmes for business rates relief and staff furlough funding. Hays Travel took the opportunity to acquire Thomas Cook because Hays had built a robust business for over forty years and had the resources to handle a significant acquisition. When a black swan event hit them, they robustly addressed the challenge. What a contrast that was to Carillion's ostrich approach to its own problems.

Simon was prescient. His book, *Administrative Behavior*, was first published in 1947 – almost half a century before wide adoption of the internet and email and, even then, he was raising the problem of information overload.

> We are all drowning in a sea of information (gasping for time), only a small amount can be attended to. What we attend to by design or

accident is a major determinate of decisions. Given scarcity of attention, how can we be more systematic to focus on the most valuable
sources of information. Agenda formation is part of attention focusing, an essential part of rational decision-making.

Simon proposed that we need to create a representation of the decision
problem. We will look at one useful representational model, the Stacy diagram, later in this section. Simon proposed that formulating a problem is
part of the problem-solving task. 'The classical view of rational decision-
making provides no explanation of where alternative courses of action origi-
nate from' and he observed that 'the planning process gives limited attention
to generating alternatives.'

Another useful device for challenging prevailing wisdom and group think
is the Israeli model that is called the Devil's Advocate Office, Red Team or 10th
Man. The name originates from the devil's advocates, officials in the Catholic
Church, whose job was to argue against sainthood during canonisation hearings.

Following the 1973 Yom Kippur War, which took Israeli intelligence by surprise, the Israeli team was established, and it can challenge prevalent assumptions and take a contrarian position within the intelligence community. The
unit is small and elite, consisting primarily of officers with academic backgrounds. One of the key elements is access. The officers have unfettered access
to information through the military and are capable of tendering reports to
senior levels, even reaching above the major general who commands military
intelligence. The combination of access to information and the ability to challenge hypotheses by going above the command chain is critical in providing a
control for intelligence reports and an antidote to group think and confirmation bias. A similar structure in the corporate world would be a powerful aid
to executive decision-making, and it would avoid members of a strategy team
being too intimidated to challenge the existing narrative.[9]

In 2004, the US military established the Red Team University within the
University of Foreign Military and Cultural Studies (UFMCS) in Fort Leavenworth,
Kansas. The school may have been closed down during the Trump presidency,
and that is perhaps predictable considering Trump's leadership style.

## Stacy Landscape Model

Professor Ralph Stacy, a British organisational theorist, developed the Stacy
diagram in the 1990s. The diagram provides a useful framework for strategic

thinking and getting a handle on policy and implementation disagreements. The model helps us move away from a one-solution answer.

The Stacy diagram has two axes. The Y-axis, Agreement, maps the level of agreement on a problem or policy. Agreement ranges from high at the graph origin to low.

The X-axis is the amount of certainty for how to solve the problem or implement the strategy. High certainty at the graph's origin is where experts agree on how to implement the strategy or solve the problem. Where there is low certainty, specialists don't know how to solve the problem.

Let's look at an example from Carillion about the contributions to the pension fund shortfall. Management had low certainty that they could meet the pension obligations or even that they had a problem, and they had low agreement on what needed to be done about the problem. The board's behaviour was uncertain, unpredictable, and disorganised. The problem sat in the top right-hand corner of the graph where there is low agreement and low certainty of a solution. Stacy labelled that area as unorganised.

Problems in the lower-left part of the graph are described as organised or the zone of order, and those problems tend to be dealt with in a more logical and disciplined way. Humans are much more comfortable with problems where there is agreement and certainty. Everyone agrees on the problem, and everyone agrees on how to solve it.

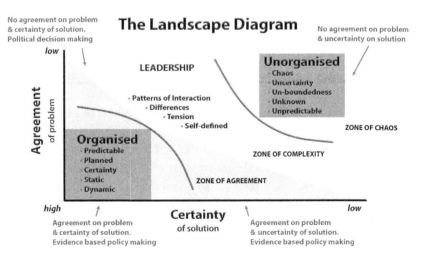

Figure 9.1 The Stacy strategic landscape model.
Source: Adapted from multiple sources.

Humans don't like uncertainty, low agreement, and conflict. They will try to avoid dealing with problems in the top right unorganised area or the zone of chaos, putting them into the too difficult category. In the zone of chaos, we don't agree on the policy or strategy problem, and we don't agree how to solve it.

In the lower right part of the graph, there is general agreement on a policy or strategy, but there is disagreement on how to solve the problem.

The upper left of the graph, the area of disagreement, is when people don't agree on a problem. If they can agree on a problem, then experts know how to solve it − but a prerequisite is to reach agreement on the problem. In this situation, different parties may want different things. This area is typical of political problems, and it is where the horse trading takes place.

The area between the upper-right zone of chaos and the area in the lower-left of agreement is called the zone of complexity. This is the area between disagreement with no solution and agreement with a solution. The area of negotiation and searching for a solution is in that central area.

The Stacy model provides a helpful way of thinking about and mapping strategic issues and any decision where a solution is elusive. Presenting the Stacy diagram as a tool to understand a problem can, in and of itself, move parties who are in disagreement towards a better understanding of the issues, and the chance of narrowing the gap is improved.[10]

## Risk and Signal Detection Theory With Type 1 and Type 2 Errors

The signal detection theory framework, despite its off-putting name, is a simple matrix to help us understand and think about risk. In our 2 × 2 matrix, we have four situations. (See figure 9.2 below) Two actions are correct, and two are errors. In the top-left box (D), there is a real risk, and we account for it so the decision is correct. In the bottom right box (B), there is no risk, and we don't account for it which is again a correct decision. The top-right box (C) may also not be too big a problem. We accounted for a risk that wasn't there, which is known as a Type 1 error. In effect, we were too cautious. The bottom-left box (A) is the greatest risk. There was a problem, we didn't account for it, and that is a Type 2 error. There are in effect three 'good' outcomes.

| | Real Risk | Not Risk |
|---|---|---|
| **Risk accounted** | Correct decision **D** Good outcome | Bad decision **C** Good Outcome False Alarm Type 1 |
| **Risk not accounted** | Bad decision Bad outcome Type 2 Error **A** | Correct decision Good outcome **B** |

Figure 9.2  Risk. Signal detection theory. Type 1 and Type 2 errors.

In the medical world, if a patient is ill and we give them appropriate medicine, this is the correct decision. If we give the medicine and they are not ill, it's probably fine, too, unless there are bad side effects, or the medicine is incredibly expensive. That is a Type 1 error. If we don't give medicine and the patient is ill, we have made a Type 2 error, and that may be a serious mistake. If we don't give the medicine and the patient is not ill, then again, we made the correct decision.

If we use the matrix of two choices of action and two situations, we get the four boxes. Let's apply this to Carillion's decision on the trade-off between paying a dividend and using cash or not paying a dividend and conserving it.

**Scenario A:** If there was a real risk of going bust by running out of cash, and the management team ignored that risk and paid out the dividends, the company would go bust which is, in fact, what happened. As explained earlier, this is the most serious error – Type 2.

There were three other possibilities:

**Scenario B:** If there was not a risk of running out of cash, and Carillion kept paying the dividend, they would have a good outcome – the CEO would keep his job, the shares would stay high, and everyone would be happy.

What if the management team were cautious? Let's call this **Scenario C:** Carillion stops paying the dividend, and there was not a deficit in the pension fund – perhaps because the investments in the fund increased in value at a higher rate than expected. The worst-case scenario of going bust would be avoided, the business would be stronger because it had bigger cash reserves, the share price might drop because there was no dividend, shareholders might demand that the CEO be replaced with someone more dynamic, and Adam would have made less money selling his share options.

In the fourth possibility, **Scenario D**, where there was a real risk of running out of cash, and the management plan for this risk was by withholding the dividend, they made the correct decision. The business doesn't go bust although, of course, the shares might go down with the possibility of disgruntled investors. As nobody would know if the business had been saved, the CEO probably wouldn't get much credit for his prudence.

I suspect that good decisions with good outcomes are more often due to luck and not skill or good judgement, but there are not many leaders who would admit to that!

Carillion made major acquisitions that carried huge pension risk. Perhaps they understood the real risk and accounted for the risk but did not account enough, or maybe the management at the time knew they would not be there to face the consequences of their folly. Remember that they were making decisions more than a decade before the collapse in different economic and political circumstances.

We will never know.

## Kahneman's Decision Models

Earlier, we looked at Daniel Kahneman's System 1 and System 2 in the section on heuristics. System 1 thinking is typified by the doer – fast, impulsive, and intuitive – someone who seizes the moment. Bravery or bravado is harnessed in advertising and politics by creating emotions and generating automatic responses. System 1 gives quick answers with little mental effort, and ambiguity is suppressed because of associative memory. Associative memory is when a difficult judgement is required and a related judgement comes easily to mind, so the easy judgement is used instead. We are often unaware of this substitution, however, substitution leads to errors because we are probably using an answer from another question.

Politicians use tricks all the time. They tell and use stories to persuade us to make a decision. If the story is coherent, then confidence in the validity of a decision is high. But that can be a big problem. Who doesn't want low taxes and economic growth? We can make a good story out of little information, and we can easily misrepresent a problem. The quality of a story doesn't depend on the quality of fact. It depends on emotional and subjective confidence.

Intuitive thinking gets better with practice, experience, and greater expertise. It's worth carefully considering when you can trust your intuition, and when you know you should be more thoughtful.

System 2 thinking is associated with the planner who uses slow, reflective, and deliberate effort that is easily impaired by other activities. With System 2 thinking, we need to pay careful attention to the problem and, for most of us, this is psychologically stressful and tiring.

When we are under the pressure of time, the quality of our decision-making is decreased. Time acts as a pressure switch, pushing us from System 2 to System 1. The skill we need is to recognise those important and expensive-to-reverse decisions that demand System 2 thinking so that we can respond appropriately.

Kahneman and fellow researchers, Lovallo and Sibony, developed a structured approach to decision-making based on addressing the problems of bias which they called Mediating Assessment Protocol (MAP). They suggest that the root cause for poor strategic decisions is that leaders fail to isolate their human biases and tendencies, and that ultimately drives them to make fewer sound decisions. Their plan for dealing with this is to put off gut-based decision-making until a choice can be informed by a number of separate factors. The key is to get as much evidence as possible before allowing yourself to decide. This approach helps us to avoid being guided by irrational factors by training ourselves to isolate and identify what information actually tells you. The next step is to identify the factors in a decision and work out how they will be assessed. By breaking down those factors, we avoid getting excited about one aspect and then glossing over the others. Intuition does have a role to play if it is well informed and does not overshadow other important factors.[11]

Kahneman expands his ideas in his book, Noise (2021). He suggests a number of techniques for noise reduction which he calls decision hygiene. The first idea is to appoint a dedicated decision observer who is trained to spot biases because most of us are poor at spotting our own biases and much better at spotting those of other people. Second is sequencing information to avoid forming answers too early in the decision process. Third is aggregating multiple independent judgements which, if done properly, is guaranteed to reduce noise significantly. Fourth is using judgement guidelines by paying more attention to people who disagree. The last idea is structuring complex decisions into smaller component parts.

Being actively open-minded, and not seeing changing your mind as a weakness, does appear to result in better decisions.

## Group Decision-making

I want to touch on group decision-making because groups have certain behavioural dynamics that we should be aware of.

It is a myth that group decisions are more considered, moderate, and wise. Research suggests the opposite. Group decisions are usually more extreme.[12] Research by James Stoner found groups encourage risky decisions and that risk shifts when a group has a risk bias in one direction. Risk can shift in either direction depending on the group's attitude towards risk. For example, a cautious person in a risky group will shift to a more risky position.

There is another problem with groups. Group members who like to offer themselves as first among equals may try to upstage other members by being more radical. With the diffusion of responsibility in a group, it is easier to be more extreme because individual responsibility is lessened. Kahneman points out that groups are subject to informational cascades. People learn and are influenced by each other in a group. Who speaks first, and who has power, can result in follow the leader, especially where there is a strong person present.[13]

Strongly cohesive groups develop robust resistance to challenges to the group. Irving Janis, a research psychologist at Yale, pointed out, 'Group think takes place when the group arrives at a bad decision because of the unwillingness or inability of its members to challenge the prevailing narrative.'[14]

Groups polarise for several reasons, including social comparison and social identity when people compare themselves to others and endorse strong cultural values to gain approval. With our desire for acceptance, we define ourselves in group terms. The more eager we are to identify with a desirable group, the more publicly we endorse the ideas of the group and conform to group norms. The group leader, especially if powerful and opinionated or a bully, will shift positions and tend to push out group members who do not share their position on risk.[15,16]

The Abilene paradox is an interesting example of a decision-making trap that can happen in a highly cooperative organisation – for example, a medical practice or a collaborative team. In the Abilene paradox, a group of people collectively decide on a course of action that is counter to the preferences of many or all of the individuals in the group. It involves a common breakdown of group communication in which each member mistakenly believes that their own preferences are counter to the group's, and they therefore do not raise objections as they want to be agreeable to the preference of other members of the group. A common phrase relating to the Abilene paradox is a desire not to rock the boat. This differs from group think in that the Abilene paradox is characterised by an inability to manage agreement.

We can avoid the Abilene paradox by understanding that it exists and recognising it. Be careful how you confirm agreement, and watch for nonverbal signs of disagreement.

## Impact of Decision and Scale of Risk

President Obama, reflecting on the raid on bin Laden's compound, said, 'One of the things you learn as president is you're always dealing with probabilities.' He told Mark Bowden,

> No issue comes to my desk that is perfectly solvable. No issue comes to my desk where there's 100 percent confidence that this is the right thing to do. Because if people were absolutely certain, then it would have been decided by someone else. And that's true in dealing with the economic crisis. That's true in order to take a shot at a pirate. That's true about most of the decisions I make during the course of the day. So I'm accustomed to people offering me probabilities. In this situation, what you started getting was probabilities that disguised uncertainty as opposed to actually providing you with more useful information.[17]

We try to quantify risk by using probabilities, but forecasting in the real world can be extremely challenging. Amos Tversky, the Nobel Prize-winning psychologist, joked that most of us have three categories when thinking about probabilities: 'gonna happen, not gonna happen, and maybe.'

## Impact

|  | 1<br>Negligible | 2<br>Minor | 3<br>Concern | 4<br>Dangerous | 5<br>Disaster |
|---|---|---|---|---|---|
| 1<br>Unlikely | 1 | 2 | 3 | 4 | 5 |
| 2<br>Low | 2 | 4 | 6 | 8 | 10 |
| 3<br>Medium | 3 | 6 | 9 | 12 | 15 |
| 4<br>High | 4 | 8 | 12 | 16 | 20 |
| 5<br>Very High | 5 | 10 | 15 | 20 | 25 |

*Probability* (Y-axis label)

Figure 9.3 Probability and impact matrix.

Perhaps more useful than trying to put a probability on a worst-case outcome is to ask what would happen if a worst case does happen. Worst cases can occur and do more frequently than we think, so we need to assess what happens if it all goes wrong and ask if we can we live with that level of exposure. We can also explore what the costs and options are to reduce or mitigate the risk.

Using a framework, we can try to get a better sense of risk and make an attempt at quantification. The framework above has the likelihood of an outcome from low to high on the left Y-axis. On the X horizontal access, the consequences are from negligible to catastrophic. Showing the scale of risk in this form helps us think through the risks of strategic options.

### Decision-making Summary

No individual decision-making process is perfect. They are all tools that you can draw on to deal with complex decision-making and help bring clarity to challenging and often paradoxical issues. On the other hand, we need to be aware of the paralysis of FOBO – the fear of better options!

Keep in mind that we are never going to get close to perfect decision-making. We want to increase the chances of making better decisions and reduce the risk of making bad or even catastrophic ones.

Earlier, we looked at paradoxical problems and how they can be used as a way to explore strategic issues. Unexpected events, although they may be alarming at the time, can be serendipitous and can provide a platform for innovation. Chance events happen frequently. Some have small impacts, and others, like the COVID-19 pandemic, have significant and fast-changing consequences. By harnessing disruption, we can use it as a springboard for an examination of strategic issues. Brainstorming to find an opportunity, rather than focusing on a problem, can yield surprising results and help navigate a new strategic landscape.

Good leaders understand that dramatic events happen more frequently than expected. They encourage maverick thinking to generate fresh ideas and new possibilities, and they retain flexibility to adapt to new threats and opportunities. They have the confidence to encourage constructive challenges through debate, to test the robustness of decisions, and to build team cohesion and talent.

## Notes

1 Benjamin Tregoe and Cynthia T. Richetti, *Analytic Processes for School Leaders* (Alexandria, VA: ASCD, 2001).
2 John Kay and Mervyn King, *Radical Uncertainty* (New York: W. W. Norton, 2020).
3 Cohen-Hatton, Sabrina. Heat of The Moment. (2019) Doubleday.
4 Kay and King, *Radical Uncertainty*.
5 "Evidence-Based Wisdom: New Way of Thinking About Thinking," http://evidencebasedwisdom.com.
6 Adapted from C. Richetti and James Sheerin, "Helping Students Ask the Right Questions," *Educational Leadership* 57 (1999).
7 www.atlassian.com/team-playbook/plays/daci.
8 H. Simon, *Administrative Behaviour*, 4th ed. (New York: Free Press, 1997), 123, 136.
9 https://usacac.army.mil/organisations/ufmcs-red-teaming.
10 Professor Robert Geyer Lancaster University.
11 D. Kahneman, D. Lovallo, and O. Sibony, "A Structured Approach to Strategic Decisions: Reducing Errors in Judgment Requires a Disciplined Approach," *MIT Sloan Management Review* (March 4, 2019).

12  Gabi Dodoiu, Roger T. A. J. Leenders, and Hans van Dijk, "A Meta-Analysis of Whether Groups Make More Risky or More Cautious Decisions Than Individuals," *Academy of Management Proceedings* (November 30, 2017), https://doi.org/10.5465/ambpp.2016.194.

13  Daniel Kahneman, *Noise* (London: William Collins, 2021).

14  I. Janis, "Groupthink: The Desperate Drive for Consensus at Any Cost," *Psychology Today* 5 (November 1971): 43–46, 74–76.

15  Robert Cialdini, *Influence: The Psychology of Persuasion* (2021).

16  CFA Article, September 2019. Adrian Furnham, Stamford Associates. London. CFA, September 6, 2019 Group polarisation and risky decisions.

17  Mark Bowden, "Interview with President Obama," *Vanity Fair*, October 12, 2012.

# 10

## STRATEGIC TOOLKIT: ADDITIONAL PERSPECTIVES

### Reflections

I want to explore some other factors that should be considered when working on strategic issues:

1.  Innovation and invention are ever-present. We may resist change, but we can be sure our competitors are searching for and harnessing new opportunities. New ideas tend to emerge in multiple places at the same time, and the window to exploit them is limited. Strategies can be defensive, focusing on what can destroy your organisation; or they can be offensive, creating strength by exploiting new opportunities. Of course, there is often some combination of the two strategies. As part of our strategic process, we need an ongoing, broad search for the new, new thing.
2.  Artificial intelligence (AI) is becoming ubiquitous, and we will examine if it has a part to play in key strategic decisions.

DOI: 10.4324/9781003457398-11

3.  Contrary to expectations, group decisions can result in worse outcomes, depending on how the group functions.
4.  Earlier, we examined the challenge of paradoxical problems. Now we will see how they can be turned from a problem into an opportunity, allowing us to gain fresh insights into the organisation.
5.  Society's expectations of a firm are shifting, and the impact of vocal and often powerful social media groups can force rapid changes in direction.

When we finally develop an agreed strategy and are ready to make changes, the next challenge is ensuring implementation. Behavioural psychology provides insights into why people resist change, and we will look at how the best laid plans can be derailed through resistance. This leads us on to a discussion of how to get things done through communication, persuasion, and acting as choice architects.

In closing, I want to share some ideas on leadership, motivation, and craftsmanship.

## Innovation

Innovation means invention, development, and commercialisation, and it is an important part of economic growth and strategic action. For all organisations, innovation is part of the strategic process, albeit at different velocities depending on the sector.

Economist, Friedrich Hayek, argued that the knowledge required to make society function is dispersed among ordinary people rather than being available centrally in concentrated form with experts.[1] To liberate the innovation process, we need to tap into ideas across a company and outside the organisation so that innovative ideas flow into our search for new opportunities.

Matt Ridley, in How Many Light Bulbs Does It Take to Change the World (2019), wrote, 'Technological innovation is a bottom-up phenomenon that emerges by trial and error among the ideas of ordinary people not something that descends from a few brilliant minds. It relies on dispersed knowledge which is not available to central planners.' If this assertion is true, then how do we harvest these innovations and feed them into the strategic planning process?

According to Amara's law,[2] we tend to overestimate the impact of an innovation in the short term but underestimate it in the long run, and we saw this clearly with the internet bubble in the late 1990s. Towards the end of the century, there was a massive flow of start-up funding for internet firms. Then, suddenly, in early 2000, the bubble burst. After a few years, however, there was enough traction, and the new technology became a global phenomenon.

Innovation is also high risk. Being too early with an idea is as dangerous as being too late. A strategic option is to buy innovation, letting the market perform the riskiest process of working out which ideas have significant potential. The upside is filtering out most of the failures, but the downside is the heavy price tag. For example, Facebook paid $1 billion for Instagram and $19 billion for WhatsApp. Microsoft paid $26 billion for LinkedIn and $7.5 billion for GitHub. Most recently, the world's then-richest man paid $44 billion for Twitter.

There is an interesting phenomenon called simultaneous invention. Most people think that Thomas Edison invented the electric light bulb, but in February 1879, Joseph Swan lit up a lecture room of 700 people using an evacuated gas bulb with a carbon filament through which an electric current passed. Edison didn't file his patent until November of the same year. Forty years earlier, in 1840, British scientist, Warren de la Rue, then age twenty-five, developed an efficient light bulb using a coil of platinum wire. In fact, more than twenty people could lay claim to inventing the electric light bulb.

Innovation can have a dramatic impact on costs. In 1800, it took the average labourer about six hours of work to pay for a tallow candle. By 1880, an hour's light from a paraffin lamp took fifteen minutes of labour, and by the 1950s, an hour of light from an electric light bulb cost just 8 seconds of work. Amazingly, with the advent of the LED bulb, it now costs about a third of a second of work to pay for it, which is a reduction in cost of 99.9 percent from the time when we used candles.

Neophobia is the fear of anything new, an unwillingness to try new things or break from routine. Organisations often attempt to stifle or punish new ideas that diverge from the cosy consensus.[3] We will discuss this in a later section on resistance.

Hayek warned in his 1943 classic, The Road to Serfdom, 'When you have regulation upon regulation upon regulation, the end of the road is the totalitarian state, tyranny, and dictatorship.'

I want to consider three forces that slow innovation. First are government policies that protect people from change but also stifle innovation. As an example, the National Coal Board, the nationalised corporation that ran the British coal industry, employed one million people working in mining in the 1950s. The government was paying people to dig for an uneconomic fuel that the country didn't really want. With a more imaginative strategy, the money of taxpayers could have been invested in retraining the workforce, supporting the exploration of alternative forms of energy, and insulating the outdated housing stock.

One almost universal response to change is to develop institutions, rules, norms, and practices that provide security and protection against the effects of change. Examples include prohibitions, restrictive trade, monopolies, and wage control.

The second of the three forces that slow innovation is the restriction of innovation using mechanisms such as guilds and trade unions. Arguments against innovation include the cost of the destructive element, the disappearance of livelihoods, and downplaying the creative spin-offs of innovation. If the idea of guilds sounds medieval, remember the battle Uber had with licensed London taxis.

Other threats to innovation include restrictive public policies and laws that hinder progress. For example, there is supranational regulation such as the EU, IP protection, patents, and monopolies. If innovation comes from the exchange of ideas, then restricting the exchange must reduce innovation.[4]

## Artificial Intelligence and Noise

Suddenly, AI is the hot topic. At one extreme, there are claims that AI will lead to the end of humanity. On the other side of the debate, it is thought that AI is merely a technical development, no different from the invention of the steam engine or the word processor, and that AI will benefit some and harm others. Obviously, AI cannot be uninvented as it is already ubiquitous. AI is a key component of Microsoft's growth strategy; it drives Google searches and Facebook content, helps cars avoid pedestrians, spots terrorists and income tax cheats, and monitors most financial transactions. From a strategic decision-making perspective, the question is how to harness the enormous power of AI while remaining cognisant of its limitations.

Recent innovations at Open AI that are backed by prominent technology executives including Elon Musk, Sam Altman, and Peter Thiel have proved so efficient at writing that the essays produced would generate top grades at the graduate level. I asked Open AI the following question: 'Is AI a useful tool in solving strategic planning problems?' Here is its answer:

> Yes, AI can be a useful tool in solving strategic planning problems. AI algorithms can be used to analyse data, identify trends, and make predictions that can help businesses make informed decisions about their strategic plans. This can help businesses optimize their operations and make more effective plans for the future. Additionally, AI can help businesses automate certain tasks and processes, which can save time and resources, and allow strategic planners to focus on more high-level strategic planning tasks.

The overuse of AI carries its dangers. As Yuval Noah Harari observed in *21 Lessons for the 21st Century*, there is a risk 'of using downgraded humans to misuse upgraded computers.' And Musk, addressing MIT students, said, 'If I had to guess at what our biggest existential threat is, it's probably AI.'

Can and should AI be harnessed for corporate strategy? One advantage of computer decision-making is that it excludes noise, something that humans are not good at. Daniel Kahneman's book, *Noise* (2022), explores the impact of noise on decision-making. Individually, we are subject to moods, the weather, personality defects and biases, and those are all things that computers are good at ignoring. However, computers are programmed by humans, and their limitations are self-evident.

Importantly, computers are good at solving puzzles and processing large amounts of data quickly. However, corporate strategy decisions are difficult to define and are mysteries without a clear good or bad answer. AI will provide useful data inputs upon which to base our decisions, but corporate strategy will remain more of an art than a science in the foreseeable future. Professionals often feel undermined by machine decisions. However, machines are not limited by Bounded Rationality and are clearly superior at rapidly processing large amounts of data.

Kahneman differentiates between bias and noise, and he believes that in the real world, 'noise is scandalously high.' Bias is the average amount of error in a decision, but noise is the variation in error. For example, a study of 1.5 million judicial decisions found that French judges were more severe on days when the local football team lost and that they were more lenient when a person was being sentenced on their birthday.

With singular decisions, it is hard to separate the noise but easier when there are recurrent decisions. Occasion noise is the variability of a decision by the same person or group, and, as we discussed earlier, groups can actually reduce the quality of decisions.

We can only speculate on the noise, in Kahneman's terms, at the top of Carillion and its impact on decisions. Richard Howson, the CEO, was constantly buffeted by noisy demands: the fickle speculation and short selling of investors; fighting to win an important contract and then realising that it might be unprofitable; chasing a large bad debt from an intractable client in a faraway country; and simultaneously maintaining the persona of a successful and confident leader.

How did noise affect the decisions of the finance director at Carillion, Richard Adam? In 2016, with retirement looming and his share options peaking in value, he did not know if the share price would hold up and maintain the value of his nest egg. And the chairman, Philip Green, with his close links to the Prime Minister, David Cameron, and Prince Harry – perhaps hoping, like many in his position, for a knighthood. Was his decision-making impacted by personal biases and noisy interruptions to rational thinking?

## Rewards and Motivation

Motivation and reward systems affect decision-making. We need to consider how decisions will be skewed by the rewards, motivations, and culture within an organisation. Is risk-taking rewarded or punished? 'Nobody got fired for buying IBM' was a popular saying in the 1970s. We should be cognisant of how an organisation's culture impacts decision-making. Does it encourage caution by offering minimal rewards for a good decision and punitive punishment for a wrong decision, so that avoiding a decision becomes the default position, or does it encourage and reward excessive risk-taking?

When it comes to motivation, there is a gap between what science is telling us and what businesses are doing. The traditional model, based on ideas proposed in the 1900s by Frederick Taylor and the school of scientific management, proposed that management should be about carrots and sticks. We reward employees for doing what we want them to do and punish them if they don't. For example, we give share options as motivation. The stick is that you don't get anything or possibly lose your job if the shares don't do well. That approach assumes that people are fundamentally lazy and demotivated and that they will only respond to rewards and punishments.

Did the rewards offered to the senior executives at Carillion motivate them? Or were the wrong behaviours rewarded, which led to the firm's eventual collapse? Rewards can distort attitudes towards risk and encourage cheating. The scandal of fake bank accounts at Wells Fargo is a good example. Rewards can crowd out good behaviour and even become addictive.

A modern approach to motivation, building on work by Maslow at MIT in the 1960s and researchers such as W. Edwards Deming, is that self- or intrinsic motivation is what we must engender in our teams. The old model based on extrinsic carrot-and-stick motivation, in their view, rarely works and often crushes motivation and creativity. As one senior executive of a Fortune 500 company said, 'If you need me to motivate you, I probably don't want to hire you.'

Money is a common traditional carrot motivator. The best way to use money as a motivator is to take it off the table – and that means paying people fairly.

Three elements are essential in order to harness more powerful intrinsic motivation: autonomy, the desire for self-direction; mastery, the urge to be better at something; and purpose, to serve something larger than ourselves. Developing a motivating and self-empowering environment should be an element of our strategic thinking. It's not a strategy in itself, but it can powerfully influence our decisions and work culture.[5]

This is an appropriate place to mention measurement and targets. There are three dangers associated with measurements. First, what is being measured tends to become the priority, crowding out other important priorities and triggering unintended consequences. The second danger is over-measuring, known as Fordism. We frequently hear about people in some professions spending so much time collecting and supplying data that they are consuming a disproportionate amount of their available productive time. The third danger is measuring the wrong things. For example, is the number of patients seen by a doctor a good measure of performance?

There is a risk of reform fatigue. People need time for new ideas to become established and for skills to mature. The risk of constant reforms is that knowledge is not converted into deep, tacit knowledge that affects our actions and behaviours. It remains superficial until the next new reform is forced upon us.

We will examine resistance to change later, but a demotivated team is hardly likely to make an effort to implement strategic change and may well be energised to frustrate it.

## Corporate Strategic Issues and Social Responsibility

Should corporate social responsibility be part of the strategy? Should we embrace the challenge of changing expectations about corporate responsibility, or should we see it as a threat to our organisation and minimise the impact through clever PR and opportunistic high-profile actions? With the power of social media campaigns to mobilise attention, is this a new chapter in the expectations of society as to how organisations must behave and, therefore, is it an opportunity to lead? Or is this a passing fashion with all the fickleness of any fashion movement?

Marcus Rashford is a star by any measure. He is a Manchester United and England team footballer and an active social campaigner. In 2021, his salary was £10.4 million and he has an estimated net worth of over £65 million. On talksport.com Rashford pledged £25,000 to support a free school meal campaign. For him, that was less than a morning's wage. His campaign for free school meals commanded national attention for his efforts, and politicians paid attention. Is his social concern something that has a major presence in his life, or is it an opportunity to embellish the Rashford brand? I have no idea, and I assume that he is generous and well-intentioned. In an age of celebrity power, however, and – with 16 million followers on Instagram, nine million on Facebook, and seven million on Twitter (X) – any issue Rashford cares about creates a level of publicity that most businesses only dream of. Social media gives Rashford a loud voice, but that is nothing compared to another footballer, Cristiano Ronaldo, with 600 million followers on Instagram alone.

The Nobel Prize-winning economist, Milton Friedman, claimed that social concerns were not the issue of businesses: 'Business are the lifeblood of our communities. They pay their taxes to solve these broader social issues. It is the role of governments to set environmental, social, and governance standards and hold companies accountable.' He said that 'the primary aim of executives should be to maximize the value created for their shareholders. Anything else is to spend someone else's money for a general social interest.'

In 2019, the US Business Roundtable redefined the objective of a business: 'The purpose of a corporation is to promote an economy that serves all Americans.' That was followed by the Davos Manifesto 2020 that made five commitments: to customers, employees, suppliers, communities, and shareholders. Note that shareholders are mentioned last, behind society at large.

So, what is the aim of a firm, and how is it likely to change over the next decade? What will be the expectations of society, and how will we meet those expectations through our strategic decisions? Climate change, social justice, gender issues, equal rights and equal opportunities, environmental impact, labour exploitation at home and abroad, monopoly and oligopoly market abuse, and international tax arrangements are some of the issues that we now must address as business leaders, and we must incorporate them into our strategic thinking.

Here are a few questions for reflection:

1.  Should companies do more than comply with the law?
2.  Is social welfare a corporate responsibility, or is it really the responsibility of the government, the community, and the family?
3.  Are we asking too much of companies?
4.  Are companies paying lip service to corporate social responsibility?
5.  How much profit should be allocated to social responsibility? Isn't that what taxes are for?

Clearly, we need to be involved in the debate over these questions, and we must adjust our vision to participate proactively. One thing we cannot do is ignore these important, high-profile, and topical issues.

## Justice and Fairness

Let me briefly mention perceptions of justice and fairness. Some strategic decisions will have adverse consequences for groups of people, and those directly and indirectly impacted will view an organisation's behaviour from a justice and fairness perspective.

When we are perceived to be acting unfairly or unjustly, there will usually be a price to pay, and the cost might not be obvious or easily measured. Most people are not attracted to working for unjust organisations, and unjust firms will find it harder and more expensive to hire the people they want or to retain them. The damage to reputation may be subtle, but over time, it is corrosive.

Nearly 100 years ago, there was a celebrated case of an American company that suddenly notified its staff that they were not allowed to disclose salaries to each other. The staff objected and supposedly walked around their building with large signs around their necks, showing their exact salaries. Pay secrecy was made illegal in the United States in 1935, and, in the United Kingdom, it is illegal under the Equality Act 2010.

Pay, like many issues, provokes strong emotions about fairness. You may recall that in 2020, the BBC was embroiled in a high-profile row over gender pay differences. Researchers in this field have distinguished between different, but often related types, of justice: (1) Distributive justice is the fairness associated with decision outcomes and distribution of resources like pay; (2) Procedural justice is the fairness of the processes that lead to decisions; (3) Interactional justice is the treatment that an individual receives as decisions are made; (4) Interpersonal justice is the perception of respect and treatment; and (5) Informational justice is the adequacy of the explanations given in terms of their timeliness, specificity, and truthfulness.[6]

As we explored earlier, organisations operate in dynamic environments. Shocks are more frequent than we expect, and sometimes radical and painful decisions must be taken. By acting fairly and transparently with compassion and humanity, leaders can make the best of challenging strategic situations.

## Challenges of Strategy

We have come full circle in our examination of strategy and decision-making. It is helpful to remind ourselves of some of the key challenges to strategy development and implementation.

Predicting the future accurately is impossible. At best, we can come up with some broad probabilities, but to estimate probabilities for future events to the decimal point is absurd, from my experience. Plus or minus 10 percent or even 20 percent is more realistic, and often a decision will be little more than a 50:50 bet — a coin toss.

Here is a recent example of a prediction that makes an absurd inference of accuracy, and you will see similar examples every day. The UK property agents, Savills plc, predicted in 2021 that UK residential house prices would increase by 13.1 percent by 2026 and, even more specifically, in the Northwest by 18.8 percent in the same time frame.[7]

Keep in mind the catalytic consequences of accidental effects. A catalyst is an event or person that causes change. Black swan events happen more often than we think, and by their nature, they are impossible to plan for. The only practical strategy is to build enough reserves to withstand a shock. The challenge is how big a shock should we be able to withstand, and that's probably where luck comes in.

The law of unintended consequences that was popularised by American sociologist, Robert K. Merton, groups unintended consequences into three types: unexpected benefit, unexpected drawback, and a perverse result where an intended solution makes a problem worse. A rather speculative example of the latter case could be that the terrorist attack of 9/11 on the World Trade Center led to the United States invasion of Iraq. That, in turn, helped to create ISIS, which stimulated the civil war in Syria. The Syrian conflict created a massive wave of refugee emigration that pushed migrants across Europe. The increased perception of large-scale immigration helped the Brexit campaigners win the EU membership referendum and pull the United Kingdom out of the European Union. A further irony is that it is more difficult to return illegal migrants to the EU country they came through because the United Kingdom no longer has return agreements in place.

Organisations are not closed systems. There is so much that you cannot control outside your internal environment, and the unpredictable may well determine if your strategic decisions are sound.

## Five Laws of Behaviour

We have looked at numerous biases and thinking traps that lead us to make poor decisions. Here are five laws to keep in mind during the decision process:

**Law 1:** The status quo bias is prevalent and epitomised by, 'Don't rock the boat' and 'We've always done it that way.' The opposite is the action bias where we want to do something, anything, rather than nothing and waiting.

**Law 2:** Newton's first law would suggest that much of our behaviour runs on autopilot like inertia. Friction is forces that get in the way of performing a behaviour and slows you down. Forces that make a behaviour more appealing, fuel or push you forward. Without friction or fuel, we tend to maintain the status quo. As an example, imagine we want to complete an acquisition. Everyone is feeling bullish, but you come along with your decision-making risk assessment tools and create friction. Will you be popular with the action now set? Along comes a gung-ho executive who says, 'Let's get on with it, it's a great opportunity.' That is fuel. When there is a balance between friction and fuel, people will tend to maintain the status quo, i.e., do nothing or follow the strongest leader. Better decisions come when there is a balance between the advocates and the detractors with healthy debate between the two.

**Law 3:** Behaviour is a function of a person and the environment. In Carillion's case, the person or persons were the CEO and the CFO. The environment was the pressure to perform in comparison to peer groups and to meet the expectations of analysts, investors, and the press. As behaviourists, we are interested in the interaction of both a person and the environment. It is useful to think about these factors when reviewing major strategic actions and ask what are the between-the-lines drivers of strategic decisions.

**Law 4:** Trade-offs, and every decision has trade-offs, together with the potential for unintended consequences and unanticipated effects which can we both good or bad, lucky or unlucky. With trade-offs, it is helpful to understand what is given up by decision and opportunity costs. It could be time or money. Weighing trade-offs is an important part of the decision-making process.

**Law 5:** Avoid mistaking luck for skill. Coin tossing offers an interesting analogy. If you have studied statistics, you will know that when you toss a coin 10,000 times, on average you deliver about fourteen heads or tails in a row. The person who achieves the astonishing fourteen heads or tails in a row, assuming they are not cheating, is not a brilliant coin tosser but just at a lucky place on the normal distribution. There are about 10,000 hedge funds so, just based on statistical probability, if the investment decisions are made by monkeys, at least one is going to have fourteen years of beating the market!

## Communicating and Implementing

Herbert Simon wrote,

> No step in the administrative process is more generally ignored, or
> more poorly performed, than the task of communicating decisions.
> Procedural manuals are promulgated without follow-up to determine
> whether the contents of the manuals are used by the individuals to
> guide their decisions. Acceptance of the plan, the final step in coor-
> dination, is acceptance by each of the organisation members of their
> part of the group plan and it is too often ignored.[8]

What can we do to increase the chances of the final steps of our strategic
plan being implemented? First, work on building your network and credibility. Getting new ideas accepted is always difficult, and the more friends and
supporters you have, the better your chance of success.

Second, carefully plan the implementation and allocate a budget for this
essential phase. Use charm, charisma, and confidence to sell your ideas.
Forcing changes on people always creates resistance.

Communication, feedback, and follow-up are important elements of getting a plan adopted. As we discussed earlier, paying attention to the strength
of a narrative helps people understand and engage with a plan. We need
to feel sufficiently convinced about the anticipated benefits in order to act.
One contributory factor explaining Carillion's failure to raise enough capital
to keep going may well have been that their narrative was weak and lacked
credibility.

The psychologist, Professor Robert Cialdini, highlights several techniques
to persuade people to accept our ideas. Of course, accepting an idea doesn't
mean it is a good one. Cialdini suggests six common ways to influence people, and they are worth remembering when you implement your strategic
plan.

Reciprocity is when people feel obliged to give back to others, and that
may be through cooperative behaviour, a gift, or a service. So give what you
want to receive. Finding common ground, being positive, and genuinely
liking people are important because we prefer to cooperate with people we
like. Particularly important for a leader is to be aware that their behaviour
is on display and that people look to their actions to determine their own.

We see that effect in celebrity branding – from the London actress, Lillie Langtry, promoting Pears Soap 150 years ago; George Clooney cooing over Nespresso; and Lady Gaga embracing the Don Perignon champagne, to name a few.

The psychological frame matters. For example, we pay attention to things that seem more important when our attention has been grabbed. People like to feel part of something bigger, part of a movement where they have a sense of belonging. When we understand something well, we perceive it as more valuable. Conversely, when we don't understand something, we become alienated from the idea.

If you are sceptical about the power of psychological persuaders, here are two examples: (1) medical student syndrome is that 70 percent of students think they have the illness they are learning about; and (2) research in a wine store found that playing German music in the background increased the sales of German wines. Behavioural and psychological factors are powerful influences, not only on our decision-making process but also on our acceptance of new ideas. Keep these factors in mind when implementing your strategy.[9]

I want to briefly mention the role of information and choice architects. Strategy development and implementation involve ensuring that there is an efficient flow of the right information to make informed decisions and that the choice process is well managed and based on sound decision principles.

The role of an information and choice architect is an emerging idea and is someone who organises and/or checks the flow of information and the context in which people make decisions. As we have learnt, managing the process of decision-making is an important function and part of the process of improving the quality of our decisions. An awareness of human psychology, cognitive biases, and irrational behaviour better prepares us to spot common errors. However, the lack of awareness of poor decision-making practices, the conflicting pressures both internal and external, and the resistance of many leaders, particularly the less able, to embrace a more professional process are all hazards. Setting the stage for the behaviour of ourselves and others to fully contribute to the development of sound strategy is certainly a laudable goal. Building into the choice architecture the processes for dissemination, implementation, and follow-up are essential steps in the process.

## Resistance to Change

We may be brilliant at communicating, intelligent in our research and review of opportunities, visionary in developing a plan, and attentive to bias, but it is important to remember that people do not like change and disequilibrium. Although change helps some people, it can harm others.

Nicolo Machiavelli's quote is worth repeating:

> There is nothing more difficult to take in hand, more perilous to conduct, or more uncertain in its success, than to take the lead in the introduction of a new order of things. Because the innovator has for enemies all those who have done well under the old conditions, and lukewarm defenders in those who may do well under the new.

When Nestle considered introducing what turned out to be the brilliantly successful Nespresso product range, the Nescafe team strongly resisted the cannibalisation of their product. Interestingly, when Nespresso was launched in 1986, the initial results were disappointing, and it took many years before sales reached 14 billion pods annually.

We have a broad range of tools to resist change, both aggressive and passive aggressive. Here are a few common ones: ritualism (we have always done it that way), passive resistance, quiet quitting, bloody-mindedness, legal recourse, refusal, whistle-blowing, social media attacks, strikes, political intervention, lobby groups, and sabotage.

Dr. Maria Kordowicz is an organisational psychologist at Nottingham University, and she writes about quiet quitting, where employees do just enough to keep up. A Gallup Global Workplace report found less than 10 percent of UK workers were engaged or enthusiastic about their work. Perhaps this was exacerbated during COVID when so many people questioned their work/life balance and the term, the great resignation, came into use.

Harvard Professor, Ranjay Gulai, has written about the way many people have 'mentally checked out, kicking back against the long-hours culture, exacerbated by a lack of trust in their organisations, and having a sense of losing control of their work decisions.'

It is clearly risky to launch strategic changes without winning hearts and minds early in the process. Be aware of those challenges. Sometimes you will win, sometimes there will be partial victories, and sometimes it will take a new team and another era for your brilliant ideas to be accepted. You need to focus on what you can control!

## The Role of Behavioural Psychology

How can behavioural psychology help us? Can we spot problems earlier? Does it help us ask better questions? Can we use it to make better decisions? Can we improve leadership skills with a deeper understanding of behavioural factors? These are the questions that this book seeks to address.

A practical way to enhance our understanding of behaviour and cognitive bias is to observe what bothers us. When do you get angry? When do you feel like quitting or being uncooperative? When emotions are aroused, that's the time to pay attention to our judgement and behaviour. It takes effort to see the world as it is and not how you wish it to be.

It is certainly helpful to understand your own and the biases of others. Some of us are intuitively good at this, but we can all sharpen our skills. You will recall that the Chief Fire Officer's research found that 80 percent of fire service professionals made mistakes that were human errors. Amazingly, 10 percent of civilian aircraft crashes are due to running out of fuel. Since a fuel gauge is prominent in an aircraft, something is clearly interfering with a pilot's risk-awareness mechanism. If we are alert to our thinking limitations and the factors that interfere with sound decision-making, many mistakes can be avoided.

When we see a potential mistake, it is important to have the confidence to speak up. Many errors in organisations could have been easily prevented if someone had been willing to tell the boss that something was wrong.[10] That is why, as leaders, we need to create space for people to speak up, and it is why the bully leader is so dangerous. James Comey tells how President Obama was brilliant at reading non-verbal communication. He sought the views of people who would normally not be invited to comment. He would ask people sitting quietly at the back of the room what they thought. In contrast, according to recent books about how cabinet meetings functioned under President Trump, cabinet colleagues were told what their decision was or should be when the president had already made up his mind.

An organisation's culture that discourages questioning and is managed by fear should be seen as a warning sign of trouble ahead. When a leader tells their group what to think and seeks applause for their own brilliance and insight, you can be sure that the quality of the decision-making process is not functioning optimally. We need executives who can speak uncomfortable truths, and that is difficult to do when your job depends on it.

To reiterate, there are practical strategies to improve our decision-making. Prepare, plan, and pre-commit to decisions. Log and monitor decisions and consequences to enhance your awareness of the decision process. Use independent people to challenge your position. Always leave time for reflection, and avoid being rushed into a decision.

## Leadership

I want to say a few things about leadership because leadership is the driving force behind strategic decisions.

There are many styles and approaches to leadership that range from consultative and empowering to dictating. There is no one approach that works, and there are examples of leaders who have achieved remarkable things using dramatically different styles. I am reluctant to use the term great leaders, for those using approaches that may be considered as outdated, inappropriate, or downright repugnant – but success is achieved in unpredictable ways.

James Comey wrote,

> Great leaders are confident and humble. They keep asking, 'What am I missing?' They are constantly wary of what they cannot see. There is a difference between intelligence (the ability to collect and report facts, solve a problem, or master information) and judgment/wisdom (to orbit a set of facts, to see it through other people's eyes, take a set of facts and move it to a different time and place, and say what the facts mean). The best organisations obsess over leadership talent. They hunt for it, test it, train it and make it part of every conversation. Great leaders are people of integrity and decency, confident enough to be humble, kind, tough, and transparent. A great leader is aware that we all seek meaning in work – what they say is important but what they do is more important.[11]

The DNA of the leader tends to get stamped on the organisation, and judicious leaders use it consciously. Arthur Andersen & Co. had a maxim. They advised, 'Manage by the facts.' Collecting data is good protection against overconfidence, and a sound approach is to actively look for data that proves you wrong rather than data that supports your position. Some leaders are transactional. That is, they just need to keep doing deals. Recognise this and the associated risks of rolling the dice.

At Carillion, the culture became toxic as the situation became desperate and leadership disintegrated. As a former Carillion executive told me, 'Discouraging any challenge became part of the culture at the top of the organisation as control from the centre increased.'

Robert Iger was the CEO of the Walt Disney Company from 2005 to 2020. It was a transformational time for the company, and Iger achieved remarkable results. His management style was very different from that of his famous predecessor, Michael Eisner. His mantra was to 'innovate or die because technology will eventually make your business model obsolete.' In his autobiography, *The Ride of a Lifetime* (2022), he writes,

> The decision to disrupt businesses that are fundamentally working but whose future is in question, intentionally taking on short-term losses in the hope of generating long-term growth, requires no small amount of courage. Routines and priorities get disrupted, jobs change, responsibilities are reallocated. People can easily become unsettled as their traditional way of doing business begins to erode and a new model emerges.

Igor talks a lot about ethics, being decent and fair, and treating people with respect. 'As a leader you are the embodiment of the company. What people think of you is what they will think of the company.' He stresses the importance of surrounding yourself with people who are good, and good at what they do, and says that when people at the top have a dysfunctional relationship there is no way that the rest of the company can function. On strategy he makes an important point, 'Long shots aren't as long as they seem.'

One common characteristic of people who achieve great things, and it is clear in Iger's case, is that they are passionate often to the point of obsession. They have remarkable resilience, and, despite setbacks, they just keep going.

## Craftsmanship and Managing Yourself

There is a classic text by Richard Sennett of Yale University called *The Craftsman* (2009). As managers and leaders, there are important lessons to be learnt from understanding the principles of craftsmanship. Craftsmen do good work for its own sake. They learn by doing, are highly motivated, and have a passionate aspiration for quality. Plato wrote, 'An aspiration for quality drives a craftsman to improve.'

It is generally recognised that to develop a skill to a high degree, it takes 10,000 hours or about three hours a day for ten years. The problem today is that we think in shorter timescales. Developing skills takes time and dedication. We need to allow time for experimentation, reflection, practice, making mistakes, and rectifying them, but how many jobs allow for that? Replacing experienced people with younger, less expensive employees is common practice and there is risk with that approach.

Craftsmen learn from frustration. They use frustration to find solutions and build competence. Sennett highlights three skills to deal with frustrating problems: (1) reformat the problem, which can lead to a leap of imagination; (2) use patience and concentration to find a solution; and (3) identify with the problem in order to find the most forgiving elements.

Craftsmen learn by taking things apart and repairing them, and that is what we have done with our analysis of the Carillion case.

It is topical to talk about a skills-based economy, and that means trained practice versus sudden inspiration. Skills take time to acquire and mature, and they are certainly not a quick fix.

The great Italian architect, Renzo Piano, explained his process: 'You start by sketching, then you do a drawing, then you make a model, then you go to reality – you go to the site – then you go back to the drawing. There is a circularity.' I think this is a useful way of thinking about the process of developing strategy and the craftsman's mindset.

We have to balance the need to finish work with doing good work, and striking that balance is subjective. Will strategy work always be a craft, or can it be replaced by an AI machine as we discussed earlier? 'The craftsman is the emblem of human individuality' and individuality is what marks innovation and progress. The machine can propose but should never command. The Austrian physicist, Victor Weisskopf, cautioned scientific technicians that 'the computer understands the answer, but I don't think you understand the answer.'

Craftsmanship doesn't mean not using tools, but it implies a deep understanding of their use. It implies using minimum force because of skills of control. There is an old saying that 'a poor workman blames his tools' and a poor leader blames everyone but themselves.

Applying the principles of craftsmanship improves our leadership and our decision-making skills. We need to take time to learn and improve, to see learning as an essential long-term process, and to have a quest to keep improving by building on experience and taking pride in our work and values.[12]

## Closing Thoughts

A French proverb has it that in all things man's choice lies not between the good and the bad but between the bad and the worse.

I will conclude, if I may, with a quotation from Socrates, who died in Athens in 399 BC: 'The truly free individual is free only to the extent of his own self-mastery, while those who will not govern themselves are condemned to find masters to govern over them.'

The traditional business school or consulting model is of limited utility. The dynamics of any organisation are complex and shifting. Nothing is static. You need vision, open-mindedness, courage, and humility to be a great leader.

In the 1990s, Carillion was an ambitious company striving to build a strong culture within a blended construction and services business. As the company grew it completed numerous complex projects and attracted many dedicated and talented people. However, twenty years later, it had lost its way. Centralisation that stifled initiative, unrealistic financial performance targets, hidden costs from bad acquisitions, and leadership out of its depth eventually led to its ultimate demise.

Does the collapse of Carillion really matter in the scheme of things? Is it just capitalism at work and the market sorting out capacity issues?

In closing, let me give you another quotation for what I think is a rather fitting summary of the challenge we all face as strategic decision-makers. The Countess Iris Origo was an aristocrat living in Tuscany during the Second World War. She kept a diary, and in 1943 she wrote, 'The truth is that we none of us have the faintest idea what is going on behind the scenes – everyone interprets such events as he has heard of in the light of his own desires.'[13]

# Notes

1  F. A. Hayek, "The Use of Knowledge in Society," *American Economic Review* 35, no. 4 (1945): 519–30.

2  Roy Amara was a Stamford University computer scientist and longtime head of the Institute of the Future. He made this insightful observation early in the 1960s, before the Internet, self-driving cars, genetic engineering, and AI, but well after observing the phenomenon with the development of the steam engine, the telegraph, and the computer.

3  Hayek, "The Use of Knowledge in Society."

4  Matt Ridley, *How Many Light Bulbs Does It Take to Change the World IEA* (2019).

5  Daniel H. Pink, "Drive: The Surprising Truth About What Motivates Us," 2009, https://selecthealth.org/wellness-resources/-/media/2B09D34BF9A A41719729C765F5F45D91.ashx.

6  Adrian Furnham, January 10, 2020, Pay Secrecy. CFA Society UK.

7  *Peer-to-Peer Finance News*, November 19, 2021.

8  H. Simon, *Administrative Behaviour*, 4th ed. (London: Free Press, 1997), 116.

9  R. Cialdini, *Influence: The Psychology of Persuasion* (2021).

10  Richard Thaler, *Misbehaving* (New York: W. W. Norton, 2015), 356.

11  James B. Comey, *A Higher Loyalty* (New York: Flatiron Books, 2018).

12  Richard Sennett, *The Craftsman* (New Haven: Yale University Press, 2008).

13  Iris Origo, "War in the Val d'Orgcia, Italy," 53, August 3, 1943, https://push kinpress.com/books/war-in-val-dorcia/.

# APPENDIX: BEHAVIOURAL BIAS CHECKLIST

Cognitive biases are patterns of thought that lead to suboptimal outcomes such as poor decisions. Most of these biases are the result of mental short-cuts, logical errors, social factors, and memory shortfalls. We all suffer from biases, and most of us have many more than we realise. A fun exercise is to read the following list and mark those biases that you have observed in other people and those that you have exhibited yourself. Try to be honest.

| | Bias | Characteristic | Observed in others | Exhibited by me |
|---|---|---|---|---|
| 1 | Above-Average Bias | A high percentage of people rate themselves as above average, which is linked to the illusion of asymmetric insight, a belief that someone has more insightful knowledge about people than people have about them. It is also linked to superior self-awareness. | | |
| 2 | Ambiguity Bias | People avoid choices that involve some uncertainty, even when a better choice is clearly available. That links to cognitive dissonance (paradox), a feeling of discomfort when two contradictory ideas are entertained at the same time. | | |
| 3 | Attitude Polarisation | The tendency to harden beliefs when challenged, which is also known as the backfire effect. | | |

(Continued)

(Continued)

|  | Bias | Characteristic | Observed in others | Exhibited by me |
|---|---|---|---|---|
| 4 | Barnum Effect | Viewing general statements as accurate and insightful for a personality or their ability. It is often used by fortune tellers, management consultants, and investment advisors. | | |
| 5 | Blind Spot Bias | The failure to recognise a cognitive bias in oneself and noticing bias much more in others. It is linked to the fundamental attribution error, which is viewing errors of other people as a result of their personal flaws but viewing one's own errors as a result of external factors. | | |
| 6 | Complexity Bias | Belief that a complex solution is better than a simple one. It is a common bias with highly intelligent people and engineers. Links to the curse of knowledge, an inability of an expert to understand or have empathy with a layperson's view of an issue. | | |
| 7 | Congruence Bias | Designing a study to confirm an hypothesis instead of challenging it. For instance, using management consultants to confirm a position. It is linked to contrast effect, a tendency for evaluations and comparisons to be influenced by context, e.g., selecting benchmarks that make performance look good, commonly used by hedge funds and politicians. | | |
| 8 | Endowment Effect | The placement of more value on what is already owned (Thaler, 2015). Links to cognitive inertia, the general tendency for beliefs to endure even in the face of mounting contradictory evidence. Also links to loss aversion and prospect theory. | | |
| 9 | Expectation Bias | This is when expectations are allowed to influence perception unconsciously. When something is expected to happen, it doesn't mean it will happen. | | |
| 10 | False Consensus Effect | Assuming people agree with you more than they do. For example, assuming that a lack of argument means agreement. It is a serious problem for arrogant bullies. | | |
| 11 | Fairness | When we think we are being treated unfairly, we do often respond irrationally. | | |

| | Bias | Characteristic | Observed in others | Exhibited by me |
|---|---|---|---|---|
| 12 | Fundamental Attribution Error | A situation where hard work is credited for success and external forces outside one's control are blamed for failures. The benefit of doubt is not extended to others. It is linked to blame transference. | | |
| 13 | Halo Effect | Assuming that someone who is good at one thing may be good at another. Charismatic leaders often benefit from this effect, blinding people to their limitations. | | |
| 14 | Illusion of Control | A tendency for a person to think they can control things that are completely out of their control. | | |
| 15 | Misremembering | If a project goes wrong, a subordinate gets the blame. If things work out, the most senior executive takes the credit. | | |
| 16 | Narrow Framing | Managerial decision-making that is driven by two countervailing, but not necessarily offsetting, biases: bold forecasts and timid choices. Links to framing effect where people view a problem depending on how the question is framed. | | |
| 17 | Outcome Bias | Judging a decision based on the outcome rather than exactly how the decision was made. Just because someone wins at the casino doesn't mean gambling was a good idea. | | |
| 18 | Ostrich Effect | Burying one's head in the sand. It is a decision to ignore dangerous or negative information. | | |
| 19 | Overconfidence Bias – Dunning Kruger | People are often overconfident. Too much confidence in one's abilities causes one to take greater risks. Experts are more prone to this bias. It is the illusion of superiority and links to hubris. Also links to the above-average effect, where most people think they are better than average. | | |
| 20 | Social Comparison Bias | Treating someone differently when they are seen as competing with one's own strengths. Manifested when a manager rejects a new hire because they might show the manager's limitations or when they have stronger leadership skills. | | |

(Continued)

(Continued)

|  | Bias | Characteristic | Observed in others | Exhibited by me |
|---|---|---|---|---|
| 21 | Sour Grapes | Based on Aesop's fable about the fox who cannot reach some grapes, so he assumes they must be sour. | | |
| 22 | Spotlight Effect | A situation where someone thinks people are considering every word when a presentation is being made but, in fact, those people are not paying much attention at all. We wouldn't worry so much about what people think of us if we realised how little they do. | | |
| **Group Think Biases** | | | | |
| 23 | Acquiescence Bias | The tendency to agree that something is true, although unsure. | | |
| 24 | Bandwagon Effect | The probability of a person adopting a belief increases as more people adopt that belief. Known as groupthink and following along with peers or celebrities. | | |
| 25 | Clustering Illusion | The tendency to see patterns in random events. Gamblers often believe in a winning streak. It is linked to illusory correlation, seeing things as related without evidence. | | |
| 26 | Choice-Supportive Bias | When something is chosen, that person tends to feel positive about it, even if the choice has flaws. | | |
| 27 | Confirmation Bias | People search to confirm evidence rather than disconfirming it. A search can be accentuated when unwarranted assumptions make some disconfirming evidence seem less likely. | | |
| 28 | Conservatism Bias | The favouritism of prior evidence over new evidence. | | |
| 29 | Creeping Normality | A significant problem that doesn't cause alarm because change happens slowly. | | |
| 30 | Discounting the Future | According to Thaler, this is not an exponential rate but a hyperbolic rate. | | |
| 31 | Escalation | Attempting to fix a bad decision by increasing one's commitment to it, also known as doubling down. | | |

| | Bias | Characteristic | Observed in others | Exhibited by me |
|---|---|---|---|---|
| 32 | Hindsight Bias (Knew it all along) | Thinking a result was inevitable after the event exacerbates misremembering bias. Links to outcome bias, judging a past decision by its outcome as opposed to the quality of the decision. Also mistakes luck for ability and views past events as more predictable than they were. | | |
| 33 | Identifiable Victim Effect | The tendency to feel greater sympathy for a single identifiable victim or a compelling story rather than statistical evidence of harm. | | |
| 34 | Investment in Management Ego | There is more of a sense of ownership when a great deal of work is put into something. When a sense of ownership exists, there is a greater fear of loss (loss aversion), so an idea or project is held onto irrationally. | | |
| 35 | Parkinson's Law of Triviality. (Bicycle shed syndrome) | Focusing on the trivial details of a complex problem because they are easier to understand. | | |
| 36 | Scope Neglect or Scope Insensitivity | A situation when someone finds it difficult to imagine large numbers of things, and they also ignore the size of a problem in an evaluation. | | |
| 37 | Slothful Induction | Resistance to reaching a conclusion despite ample evidence for it. | | |
| 38 | Status Quo Bias | Forces that inhibit change. Inertia and a strong preference for things to remain the same. | | |
| 39 | Zero-Risk Bias | People love certainty, even if it is counterproductive. Eliminating risk means eliminating harm, and it can mean devoting excessive resources to reduce a particular risk. | | |
| **Muddy Thinking Biases** | | | | |
| 40 | Action versus Inaction | There is sometimes pressure to act in times of uncertainty or volatility, and sometimes there is inaction due to fear. This is linked to the capitulation bias when someone acts irrationally because of panic caused by movement of the herd. | | |

(Continued)

(Continued)

|  | Bias | Characteristic | Observed in others | Exhibited by me |
|---|---|---|---|---|
| 41 | Anchoring Bias | Overreliance on the first piece of information that is heard. The first offer establishes the range, e.g., focusing on return without counterbalance of thinking about risk. | | |
| 42 | Attribute Substitution | Attempting to solve a complex problem with a heuristic attribute that is an incorrect substitution. | | |
| 43 | Availability Heuristic | An overestimation of information that is available or in memory and that is perhaps reinforced by recent media attention or because of its bizarreness. | | |
| 44 | Base Rate Fallacy | Valuing specific information over general information because the specific idea or story can be related to, although the specifics may not represent the population behaviour. | | |
| 45 | Begging the Question | This is a type of circular reasoning that assumes the conclusion of an argument and proves a conclusion by itself. It may take the form of an attempt to prove a statement with a synonym, e.g., that a major contract is significant because of its scale. | | |
| 46 | Breakeven Effect | More risks are taken when losses are made and there is a chance of breaking even. Pay close attention when employees are losing a lot of money. People threatened with big losses who have a chance to break even are often willing to take big risks. | | |
| 47 | Cognitive Ease | This is when an idea is dismissed because it is badly presented or because it is being sold with a jazzy presentation instead of good content. | | |
| 48 | False Analogy | Assuming that two things are similar because they share some of the same characteristics, they might be quite different in other, more significant ways. This links to a false dilemma, viewing a situation as having only two options when there may be many others. | | |
| 49 | Hasty Generalisations | Generalisations that are based on insufficient evidence. | | |

| | Bias | Characteristic | Observed in others | Exhibited by me |
|---|---|---|---|---|
| 50 | Hot-Cold Empathy Gap | People underestimate how hot or cold emotional states affect them. Hot: angry, tired, hungry. Cold: calm and collected. | | |
| 51 | Gambler's Fallacy | This is assuming that statistically independent events are related. Linked to lucky streak, the belief that someone who is lucky has a greater chance of being more lucky. | | |
| 52 | Information Bias | Tending to seek information when it does not affect action. More information is not always better. Sometimes predictions are more accurate when they are made with less information. | | |
| 53 | Loss Aversion | Prospect theory – when losses loom about twice as large as gains. | | |
| 54 | Mental Accounting | People think of value in relative rather than absolute terms. They derive pleasure not just from the value of objects but also from the quality of the deal. | | |
| 55 | Momentum | The irrational behaviour of momentum relies on the assumption that current winners keep winning and losers keep losing. The winners get overbought, and the losers get beaten down further. This is linked to the tendency to extrapolate recent gains, and it partly explains financial bubbles. Linked to the fear of missing out and the desire to get on the bandwagon. | | |
| 56 | Not Invented Here | Organisation preference to create things independently when external alternatives are available more cheaply or faster. | | |
| 57 | Optimism Bias | Overestimating the probabilities of positive things and underestimating the probability of risks. Related to pessimism bias or overestimating difficulty or risk. | | |
| 58 | Placebo Pricing Effect | Pricing a product at a higher price to make it appear better, and the buyer believes that it works better than the same discounted product. | | |
| 59 | Pro-Innovation Bias | A proponent of an innovation overvalues its usefulness and undervalues its limitations. | | |

(Continued)

(Continued)

| | Bias | Characteristic | Observed in others | Exhibited by me |
|---|---|---|---|---|
| 60 | Recency Bias | The latest information is weighted more heavily than older data. For example, investors think the market in the future will look more like it does today. | | |
| 61 | Quantitative Bias | Overemphasis on numbers while missing the qualitative data. | | |
| 62 | Salience Bias | People focus on the most easily recognisable features of a person or a concept. For example, when an idea resonates with a similar experience whether good or bad. It links to trust bias. | | |
| 63 | Selective Perception | Allowing our expectations to influence how we perceive the world. It is related to cherry picking, choosing information that supports an idea while ignoring contrary information. It is also related to the focusing effect, which focuses too heavily on a single aspect of a decision or problem. It filters information according to a particular viewpoint. | | |
| 64 | Sharpshooter Fallacy | A goal is changed to match the results. For example, when a sharpshooter names his target after taking the shot. This is not uncommon in politics. | | |
| 65 | Statistics and Ignorance | There is sometimes insensitivity to sample size and statistical validity. This is related to being impressed by numbers, even if they are invalid or wrong. Linked to inferring accuracy when numbers may only be as accurate as the weakest data. Also linked to quantitative bias. | | |
| 66 | Stereotyping | Expecting a group or a person to have certain qualities without real information to support that view. It is useful for allowing people to assess situations quickly, but it is often overused and can be unreliable. | | |
| 67 | Sunk Costs (Sunk cost fallacy) | When an amount of money has been spent and the money cannot be retrieved, money is said to be sunk. Economic theory would suggest that, in general, these costs should be ignored. This is related to loss aversion, a strong preference for avoiding losses over acquiring gains. | | |

| | Bias | Characteristic | Observed in others | Exhibited by me |
|---|---|---|---|---|
| 68 | Survivorship Bias | There is a focus only on survivor data, and discounting or ignoring a situation if all of the samples had been included. | | |
| 69 | Trust Bias | Trust bias is when someone overpays for something because of familiarity. It is seeing ourselves in the other person, or what we like about them. | | |
| 70 | Well-Travelled-Road Effect | Underestimating familiar tasks and overestimating the unfamiliar. | | |
| 71 | Worse than Average Effect | People think they are worse than average at tasks when they find them difficult to master. | | |

# BIBLIOGRAPHY

Andersson, Ola, Håkan J. Holm, Jean-Robert Tyran, and Erik Wengström. "Risking Other People's Money: Experimental Evidence on Bonus Schemes, Competition and Altruism." *The Scandinavian Journal of Economics* 122 (March 18, 2019).

Ariely, Dan. *Predictably Irrational.* New York: Harper Collins, 2010.

Branham, Leigh. *Keeping the People Who Keep You in Business.* New York: American Management Association, 2000.

Cantril, Hadley. *The 'Why' of Man's Experience.* New York: Macmillan, 1950.

Chakravarty, Sujoy, Glenn W. Harrison, Ernan E. Haruvy, and E. Elisabet Rutström. "Are You Risk Averse Over Other People's Money?" *Southern Economic Journal* 77 (2011): 901–13.

Cialdini, Robert. *Influence: The Psychology of Persuasion.* New York: Harper Business, 2021.

Cohen-Hatton, Sabrina. *Heat of the Moment.* London: Doubleday, 2019.

Comey, James B. *A Higher Loyalty.* New York: Flatiron Books, 2018.

de Wit, Bob. *Strategy: An International Perspective.* 7th ed. 2020 Working Paper 10813. Cambridge, MA: National Bureau of Economic Research, September 2004.

Dodoiu, Gabi, Roger T. A. J. Leenders, and Hans van Dijk. "A Meta-Analysis of Whether Groups Make More Risky or More Cautious Decisions Than Individuals." *Academy of Management Proceedings* (November 30, 2017). https://doi.org/10.5465/ambpp.2016.194.

Frederick, Shane. "Cognitive Reflection and Decision-making." *Journal of Economic Perspectives* 19 (2005): 25–42.

Haldane, Andrew G., and Robert M. May. "Systemic Risk in Banking Ecosystems." *Nature* 469 (2011): 351–55.

Hamilton, Nigel. *War and Peace: FDR's Final Odyssey: D-Day to Yalta, 1943–1945.* Mariner Books, 2019.

Handy, Charles. "Educating for Uncertainty." *London Business School Review* 3 (2018).

Handy, Charles. *The Second Curve.* London: Random House, 2015.

Haselton, Martie G., and Daniel Nettle. "The Paranoid Optimist." *Personality and Social Psychology Review* 10, no. 1 (2006): 47–66.

Hayek, Friedrich A. "The Use of Knowledge in Society." *American Economic Review* 35, no. 4 (1945): 519–30.

House of Commons. *Business, Energy and Industrial Strategy and Work and Pensions Committees.* London: House of Commons, May 16, 2019.

Janis, Irving L. "Groupthink: The Desperate Drive for Consensus at Any Cost." *Psychology Today* 5 (November 1971): 43–46, 74–76.

Joa-Longartt, Mylene. "EMBA Student Bayes." 2021. https://uk.linkedin.com/in/mylene-joa-longartt-5150b47.

Kahneman, Daniel. "A Perspective on Judgment and Choice: Mapping Bounded Rationality." *American Psychologist* 58, no. 9 (2003): 697–720.

Kahneman, Daniel. *Noise: A Flaw in Human Judgement.* New York: Little, Brown Spark, 2021.

Kahneman, Daniel, Dan Lovallo, and O. Sibony. "A Structured Approach to Strategic Decisions: Reducing Errors in Judgment Requires a Disciplined Approach." *MIT Sloan Management Review* (March 4, 2019).

Kahneman, Daniel, and Dan Lovallo. "Timid Choices and Bold Forecasts: A Cognitive Perspective on Risk Taking." *Management Science* 39, no. 1 (1993): 17–31.

Kahneman, Daniel et al. *Judgement Under Uncertainty: Heurisitcs and Biases.* Cambridge University Press, 1982.

Kay, John, and Mervyn King. *Radical Uncertainty.* New York: W. W. Norton, 2020.

Keynes, John Maynard. *The General Theory of Employment, Interest and Money.* Cambridge: Harcourt, Brace and Company, 1936.

Lefebvre, Mathieu, and Ferdinand M. Vieider. "Risk Taking of Executives Under Different Incentive Contracts: Experimental Evidence." *Journal of Economic Behaviour and Organization* 97 (2014): 27–36.

Malmendier, Ulrike, and Geoffrey Tate. *Who Makes Acquisitions? CEO Overconfidence and the Market's Reaction.* Working Paper 10813. Cambridge, MA: National Bureau of Economic Research, September 2004.

Origo, Iris. "War in the Val d'Orgcia, Italy." August 3, 1943. https://pushkin press.com/books/war-in-val-dorcia/.

Pascale, Richard T. "Co-Author of the Art of Japanese Management." 1981. https://books.google.com/books/about/The_Art_of_Japanese_Management.html?id=0064AAAAIAAJ.

Pink, Daniel H. "Drive: The Surprising Truth About What Motivates Us." 2009. https://selecthealth.org/wellness-resources/-/media/2B09D34BF9AA41719729C765F5F45D91.ashx.

Raynor, Michael. *The Strategy Paradox*. New York: Crown Business, 2007.

Ridley, Matt. *How Many Light Bulbs Does It Take to Change the World*. London: IEA, 2019.

Robson, David. *The Intelligence Trap: Why Smart People Do Stupid Things*. New York: Hodder and Stoughton, June 2019.

Simon, Herbert. *Administrative Behaviour*. 4th ed. London: Free Press, 1997.

Simonson, Itamar, and Barry M. Staw. "De-Escalation Strategies: A Comparison of Techniques for Reducing Commitment to Losing Courses of Action." *Journal of Applied Psychology* 77, no. 4 (1992): 419–26.

Smith, Wendy, and Marianne Lewis. *Both/and Thinking: Embracing Creative Tensions to Solve Your Toughest Problems*. Boston: Harvard Business Review Press, 2022.

Steer, Tim. *The Signs Were There*. UK: Harper Collins, 2021.

Taleb, Nassim Nicholas. *The Black Swan: The Impact of the Highly Improbable*. New York: Random House, 2008.

Thaler, Richard. "Anomalies: Saving, Fungibility, and Mental Accounts." *Journal of Economic Perspectives* 4, no. 1 (Winter 1990).

Thaler, Richard. *Misbehaving*. New York: W. W. Norton, 2016.

Tversky, Amos. "Elimination by Aspects: A Theory of Choice." *Psychological Review* 79, no. 4 (1972): 281–99.

Vermeulen, Freek. *Business and the Icarus Paradox*. Boston: Harvard Business Review, March 4, 2009.

Waldman, Ari Ezra. "Rational Disclosure and the Privacy Paradox." November 2019. www.behaviouraleconomics.com.

World Economic Forum. "Future of Jobs 2020." *World Economic Forum, Klaus Schwab, the Fourth Industrial Revolution*, January 2016. https://www3.weforum.org/docs/WEF_Future_of_Jobs_2020.pdf.

Yourcenar, Margaret. *Memoirs of Hadrian*. New York: Farrar, Straus and Giroux, 2005.

# ABOUT THE AUTHOR

 **Professor Jeremy N. White** has over forty years of experience in technology and venture capital financing in Europe and the United States and has been involved in over fifty acquisitions while raising more than £100 million in development capital for his companies.

Professor White founded one of the first e-commerce companies in the United Kingdom. He took that company public on the London Stock Exchange in 2000 with a market capitalisation of £250 million. He has served on the boards of a number of quoted and private companies in addition to numerous government committees. He was Deputy Chairman of the HRH Prince's Business Trust, and he is a member of the board of Pepperdine University in California.

White has an MBA from Bayes Business School and an MA in psychology from Pepperdine University. He is currently an honorary visiting professor at Bayes Business School in London, where he teaches behavioural corporate strategy to postgraduate students as well as serving on the global advisory board.

# INDEX

Printed in the United States
by Baker & Taylor Publisher Services